Editor
Patricia Miriani Sima

Editorial Project Manager
Karen J. Goldfluss, M.S. Ed.

Editor-in-Chief
Sharon Coan, M.S. Ed.

Art Director
Elayne Roberts

Associate Designer
Denise Bauer

Cover Artist
Larry Bauer

Production Manager
Phil Garcia

Imaging
Daivd Bennett
Ralph Olmedo, Jr.

Publisher
Mary D. Smith, M.S. Ed.

S0-ADY-643

Using the Newspaper to Teach Reading Skills

Challenging

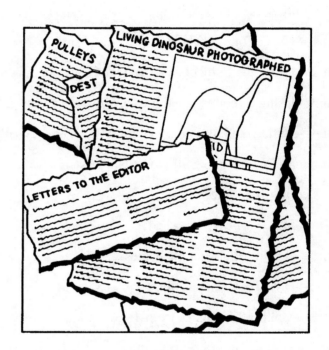

Author

Debra Carney

Teacher Created Resources, Inc.
6421 Industry Way
Westminster, CA 92683
www.teachercreated.com

ISBN-1-55734-467-1

©1996 Teacher Created Resources, Inc.
Reprinted, 2005
Made in U.S.A.

Teacher Created Resources

Table of Contents

Introduction

How To Use This Book

Using the Newspaper to Teach Reading Skills is divided into four chapters:

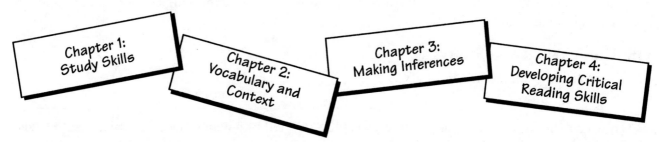

Chapter 1:
Study Skills

Chapter 2:
Vocabulary and
Context

Chapter 3:
Making Inferences

Chapter 4:
Developing Critical
Reading Skills

Each chapter is divided into four or five related lessons. Each individual lesson contains an easy to understand explanation of the skill being taught as well as examples. Following the lesson is an exercise requiring the students to read an article and answer related questions. Students are given the opportunity to work with a real newspaper with the Practice Using Your Newspaper and Now Try Your Newspower activities. Below is a more in-depth look at each component of this book. The instructions are directed to the students.

How the Lessons Are Organized

1. **Lessons.** Read the introduction to the chapter and go on to Lesson 1. Read the lesson and all of the sample news articles carefully. Think about each sample news article in the way that is suggested in the lesson.

2. **Exercises.** Do the exercises. The exercise is a longer news article followed by questions. The questions help you check to see if you have understood the lesson.

3. **Practice Using Your Newspaper.** After each lesson you are given a chance to practice the skills you have learned by using articles from your newspaper. After you have tried your skills with the newspaper, you may want to try using the same skills in the same way with one of your schoolbooks. The reading-study skills you learn apply to all kinds of reading, not just to newspaper reading.

4. **Now Try Your Newspower.** Be sure to try your "newspower" at the end of each lesson. You will be working on your own with these assignments. Doing a good job here is the best way to prove to yourself how expert you are becoming in the art of study, reading and learning.

This book may be followed in the order presented for a thorough unit on reading skills, or individual chapters and lessons may be used in isolation to fit class and individual student needs.

Chapter 1: Study Skills

Preview Questions

Think about the following questions, write your answers, and then discuss them with others. This will help you take a new look at the way you study now, and will start you thinking about ways to improve your studying in the future.

Where and When You Study

1. Describe the place where you study. _____
   _____

2. How can you improve the place where you study? Or, tell of a better place you might go to study.
   _____
   _____

3. When is the best time for you to study? Explain why. _____
   _____

4. How many hours do you study each day? _____ Each week? _____

5. Do you think you should study more than you do? Explain your opinion. _____
   _____

How You Study

6. Make a list of the different things you do when you study-read, take notes, review, etc.
   _____
   _____

7. What might you do to improve the way you study now? _____
   _____

Reviewing for Tests

8. How do you prepare for tests? _____
   _____

9. What are some things you might do to improve the way you study for tests? _____
   _____

Taking Tests

10. What are some reasons for studying, besides having to prepare for tests? _____
    _____

11. Tell which are your "favorite" kinds of tests, and tell why they are your favorites. _____

12. How do you feel as you are sitting to take a test? Do your feelings interfere with your ability to do well? _____
    _____

Whenever you sit down to read, you are also sitting down to learn. This is true no matter what the reading is–a novel, a newspaper, a magazine article, a comic strip, a textbook, or even the label on a bag of cookies.

Written words are always a message from one person to another–just as spoken words are. So the very act of reading–reading anything–means you are learning what the message is the author has set down for you.

School books, especially, provide a teaching message. It is your job as a student to learn what your books have to teach. From time to time you are tested to see how much you have learned from your reading. No one can say this is an easy job. Learning from what you read requires effort, concentration, thought, questioning, discussion and practice–the same sort of effort you put into any job you do. In fact, learning and doing well in school is much more a result of good working habits than it is a result of being a "brain" or a "genius."

The great inventor Thomas Edison said, "There is no substitute for hard work." And to those who would call him a genius, he had this to say: "Genius is one percent inspiration and ninety-nine percent perspiration." Genius, in other words, is mostly a matter of hard work. The same applies to reading, studying, and learning. Even if you do not consider yourself a genius, you can still do outstandingly well in school and go on to achieve success in any career you choose. But you must invest the perspiration it requires for studying and learning.

This chapter provides tips and guidelines for becoming a more efficient studier and learner. Other chapters tell you how to be a better, more efficient reader, which is an essential part of any study reading, of course. But now you will concentrate on such things as getting organized to study, finding a time and place, working efficiently, and reviewing and preparing for the different kinds of tests you are asked to take.

Get Organized: Choose a Time and Place

Any task becomes easier when you do it in an organized way. This is especially true for the job of studying. If you set up and stick to an organized study routine—one that works for you—you will find studying easier, and you will soon see results in the form of better grades.

To begin with, find a study nook at home which you can use regularly. Then equip it with study supplies–pencils, paper, dictionary, and so on. A great deal of time can be wasted just looking for things. And it interferes with your train of thought–your concentration.

Make sure you have good lighting directly above your work, or coming over your shoulder. Avoid both dark shadows and bright glare. Sit in a comfortable, upright chair. It is not a good idea to study while lying on a couch or bed. It is too easy to fall asleep.

Whatever study place you choose should be quiet and free of distractions. You will hear people say, "I concentrate better with the radio or TV on." Not so! This might make study time more pleasant, but it interferes with the learning process.

Read, Study, Learn

Are you a morning person or an evening person?

Before you choose a time to study, ask yourself when you are most alert. Some people are "morning people" and study best when they first get up. This means rising early, however–not studying while you brush your teeth and eat breakfast. Others are at their best later in the day or evening.

Take advantage of free or study periods you may have in school. Don't waste this valuable chunk of time. Tune out your neighbors and get down to work. A quiet library is a good place to study, too.

If you study after school or in the evening, take a break or nap for half an hour before starting. You'll need to clear your head, relax, and freshen up in order to be in the mood for serious work. Thomas Edison was able to work around the clock for days at a time. His secret? Naps. When he felt his concentration lagging, he would curl up on a handy couch, or even on the floor. It will work for you, too, when you are tired after school, sports, or other activities. But set an alarm so you don't oversleep!

No matter what time you choose, make the best possible use of it. Don't let friends interrupt you. And don't interrupt yourself with tasks and chores that somehow get left till the last minute. This usually means scheduling your activities, and sticking to your schedule as closely as possible.

Time Management

Because you have different things to do each day at different times, you should keep a calendar, just as executives and other busy people do.

Plan ahead as much as you can–for a whole week, if possible. That way, you can allow in advance for special events. For instance, if Tuesday evening features a TV special that can't be missed, homework can be scheduled for another part of the day. Once you have made up your schedule, stick to it. Learn to say "No" when your schedule is full and something else comes along.

Rule of Thumb: 1 class period = 1/2 hour homework

It is usually suggested that you spend at least a half hour at homework for each hour you spend at school. This works out to about twelve hours of homework a week. This is a minimum. At exam time or when you are having problems with a subject, you would expect to spend more time studying.

Once again, you have to plan your time. Troublesome subjects should get more time. If you find yourself with an easy history schedule one week, this time should be given to another subject. In other words, the twelve-hour block of time you give to studying each week should be used only for studying.

You will find you can accomplish more if you divide your study time into twenty or thirty-minute periods with short breaks in between. Stand up and stretch. Get a snack and a drink. But be sure to set a time limit. Five or ten minutes is enough to refresh yourself. Avoid starting activities that will distract you or be hard to leave. Don't turn on the TV or pick up a novel you can't put down again.

Ready Study, Learn

Setting Goals

Set goals for your study time. Decide on a reasonable learning goal for each subject and do your best to accomplish that goal. For instance, if your history assignment is to read Chapter 7, then that is your goal for that study period. If your English assignment is to write a composition, then your goal might be to make an outline first.

When you are finished, be honest with yourself. Did you really accomplish what you set out to do? Or did you do the least possible work in order to say you "did what the teacher said to do?" If you race through ten pages of history, zip through ten math problems without checking the answers, and answer five essay questions on an English assignment without really thinking about them, you are not studying effectively. You are not accomplishing goals. Remember, your overall goal is to learn.

A Summary of Tips for Organizing a Study Routine

1. Find a place where you can study regularly.

2. Avoid distractions such as TV, radio, or loud talk.

3. Choose a time to study when you are alert.

4. Schedule your time. Be sure your schedule allows at least 12 hours a week for studying.

5. Divide your time wisely among subjects. Put in overtime before tests or when you are having trouble.

6. Set goals for each day's work. Accomplish what you set out to do.

7. Work for twenty or thirty minutes at a time. Take short breaks in between.

8. Be flexible. Everyone's situation changes from time to time. If you get off schedule, reorganize and start again.

Practice What You Have Learned

Fill in the Personal Time Management Schedule on page 8. To do this, you must plan your school and after-school time for one week. Show when you will do studying for each of your subjects. Be sure to schedule at least 12 hours of studying in all. Also write in sports practice, music lessons, or other activities that you must allow time for. Use pencil so you can erase and juggle activities. Then, be sure to follow your schedule as closely as possible.

Read, Study, Learn

Time Management Plan for _____

Name _____

	Monday	Tuesday	Wednesday	Thursday	Friday	Saturday	Sunday
8 am - 9 am							
9 am - 10 am							
10 am - 11 am							
11 am - 12 pm							
12 pm - 1 pm							
1 pm - 2 pm							
2 pm - 3 pm							
3 pm - 4 pm							
4 pm - 5 pm							
5 pm - 6 pm							
6 pm - 7 pm							
7 pm - 8 pm							
8 pm - 9 pm							

Exercise A

Do this exercise at a time and place where you can do the best job of studying. Concentrate on reading the article. Read it only once, and then answer the questions without referring to the article. Finally, complete the Study Report on page 10.

Veterinary Medicine Demands Dedication

by Alberta Redford

Being a doctor of veterinary medicine is not all cute animals and furry friends, according to Dr. Roberta Nichols. She has had a general veterinary practice for more than fifteen years. "A critically sick or injured animal is not cute," she points out. "But it needs all the concern and professional knowledge you can give it."

It takes both dedication and determination even to be admitted to a school that trains veterinarians. Not many universities have veterinary colleges. Competition is stiff for the few places available in freshman classes.

High school preparation is much the same as is for students planning any medical career. Lots of science is called for, including chemistry and physics as well as biology. Three years of math is recommended. Because of the competition for places in schools, prospective vets will need strong grades in all their subjects.

Seven or eight years of college are required for a DVM (Doctor of Veterinary Medicine) degree. Then, you can expect to intern or work for a practicing vet for two or three years. Not until then are you really qualified to go into practice on your own.

There are a number of specialists in veterinary medicine. The largest specialty is in small animals, simply because

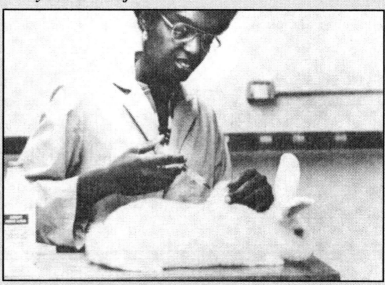

Veterinarian treating a patient.

there are so many pets that need looking after. In rural areas a large animal practice is an important specialty. This covers most of the animals you might find on a farm. It requires considerable travel since it isn't possible to bring a sick horse or cow to the vet's office. The vet has to go to them. Some large animal specialists have an equine practice and treat only horses. You will always find one or more equine specialists where race horses are bred, or where riding is a popular sport.

More and more vets are specializing even further, just as people doctors do. There are surgeons, neurologists (for diseases of the nervous system),

and orthopedic surgeons (bones and muscles).

There are even a few psychiatrists who treat dogs and cats with personality problems.

It takes a very special kind of person to be a veterinarian. Animal patients do not understand why the doctor is treating them. Sick or well, they would rather be left alone. Instead of thanks for making a patient well, a vet is just as likely to get nipped, scratched, or kicked, if he or she is not careful. The loving licks belong to the animals' owners.

And it's the owners who are grateful to a good veterinarian who gives them back a well pet.

Read, Study, Learn

Exercise A *(cont.)*

Questions

1. Why is it difficult to get into a veterinary school? _____

_____

_____

2. You would certainly study biology if you want to work with animals. What other subjects are mentioned in the article? _____

_____

3. What kind of animals does a doctor with an equine practice treat? _____

_____

4. If your pet suffers a broken leg, what kind of specialist can provide the most expert treatment?

_____

_____

5. Fill in the blanks: If your dog hides under the bed frequently and growls at you, you could say he has a _____ problem, and you might take him to an animal

_____

Study Experience Report

1. What place and what time did you choose to study Lesson 1 and do Exercise A? _____

_____

2. Explain why you think this was the best time and place for you to study. Or, tell why it was not, and where and when you would prefer to study another time. _____

_____

_____

3. Once you have decided where and when to study, what sorts of things seem to interfere with your schedule? _____

_____

_____

4. Discuss with other people ways that you can fit at least 12 hours of studying, per week, into a schedule with all of the other things you have to do. _____

_____

_____

Read, Study, Learn

Now Try Your Newspower: Option 1

Set a goal of reading as much of the newspaper as you can. Allow one hour for this, and read the paper in your quiet study place.

Focus on articles you find interesting, and read at least one article on every page. (If your newspaper is a small one, read more articles and advertisements. If it is a large newspaper, read fewer articles).

Now Try Your Newspower: Option 2

Find a rather long article about your favorite sport in the sports section of your newspaper. Choose an article that explains why the losers lost as well as why the winners won.

After losing a game, the losers' coach has to plan the players' "homework and study" schedule to prepare for the next "test" or competition. For example: a losing football team may have to study, review and practice its defensive plays. A pitcher may have to work on his fast ball. A tennis player may have to study and practice her serve.

Pretend you are the coach. Write a detailed outline that tells how your team or player will "study" and do "homework" in order to win the next game.

In your outline, remember you have to prepare players mentally to win. That is, you have to put them in a winning frame of mind–convince them that they can win. Tell how you would do this as well as telling what plays or moves must be practiced.

Answer the following question on the lines below: How is an expert athlete practicing a sport like a student studying schoolwork?

Don't think of studying as something you do only for a test. Studying also includes preparing for the next day's classes and discussions. Think of studying as an ongoing process. You *study* throughout the year. You *review* for a test.

The first step of the studying process takes place while you read.

Marking and Making Notes

Marking main ideas and important points as you read, or making notes about them, is an important study technique. It helps you concentrate on what is most important in your reading. In addition, it becomes a ready-made review outline for quizzes and tests. Decide what is important in a paragraph, underline it, and perhaps make yourself a brief note in the margin. Don't mark too much, or you will only succeed in confusing yourself.

Of course, if your books are loaned to you by your school, you cannot mark in them. But you can keep a list of main ideas and important details on a separate sheet of paper. These will be just as useful to you as would marked items in your books.

Here is one way to mark a paragraph, or make notes about it:

Another weapon of the whites against Native Americans was something they did not use on purpose. Indeed, the whites feared it themselves. This was disease. Smallpox, measles, and other sicknesses may have wiped out as many as half the Western Native Americans. This happened years before the final great battles ever took place. The germs traveled with traders and so preceded the settlers by decades. The Native Americans had no inherited resistance or immunity to many diseases of the whites, since the germs had been "imported" from Europe. Native Americans died by the band and even by the tribe for sicknesses that only made most whites uncomfortable.

Disease as a Weapon

The important idea here is that the white man's diseases became a weapon against the Native Americans. An important detail is that the Indians had no immunity, or protection, from these "imported" germs. Thus, your notes could look like this:

Disease as a weapon against Native Americans

—Native Americans had no resistance or immunity to many diseases.

If you continue this way for the rest of the chapter, you will force yourself to think carefully about each important idea. And, in addition, you will have a good outline to use for review.

How To Study

Questions and Comments

Besides marking main ideas and details, you should get into the habit of writing down questions about things you do not understand. You should also write down any comments you have about the material. These are things to bring up in class the next day.

For example, after reading about the Native Americans, your list of questions and comments might look like this:

1. How was white civilization different from Native American civilization?
2. Is one way of life better than another way of life?
3. The Native Americans were at a terrible disadvantage.

Some questions are easy to answer. Others have no final answer. They can only be discussed. But the simple act of questioning and discussing is, in itself, a learning process. This happens in the classroom. It is the reason why so many teachers insist on classroom participation.

Classroom Participation

Classroom participation is a vital part of studying. Many teachers, in fact, consider it an important part of your grade. Here is why:

1. Talking about something helps you to understand it better.
2. Misunderstandings are cleared up.
3. Different points of view are revealed.
4. New ideas come out of discussions.

This is what goes on in clubs, in committees, in town meetings, in support groups–in every gathering where decisions are made and problems are dealt with. Being able to take part in a discussion is a vital life skill. That is why teachers insist on it.

At the same time, it is a valuable study aid. Participating in class keeps you alert. It helps fix information in your mind. And it gives you a better feeling for the subject.

Do a Little More Than You Have To

After you have read your assignment, noted important points and jotted down any questions you have, you should do a little more. If there are practice problems in your textbook, do them! If there are sample questions, answer them! This is what will give you an extra edge. Top-seeded athletes are tops because they give their sport more than they have to. People who are successful in business or in the arts are successful because they put in more than they have to.

If you do what is assigned, plus a little more, you will understand more of your work. If you understand more, you will perform better in school.

Exercise B

As you read through this story, mark or write down the main ideas and important details. Share your responses with other members of the class to see if you agree on what the main ideas and details are.

Motorcycle Safety Rodeo Held

MARSHFIELD—The Fourth Annual Motorcycle Safety Rodeo was held here this weekend. Over fifty participants attended the day-long competition in motorcycle handling.

The goal of the rodeo was to promote safe motorcycle riding habits. Motorcycle riding is one of the most popular activities in America today. However, there is no denying the dangers associated with riding a motorcycle. A driver is more vulnerable to injuries because he or she is less protected than a driver in a car. Safe motorcycle riding habits can cut down the chances of accidents and injuries.

The Rodeo included workshops on braking, shifting, maintenance, and protective gear and clothing.

"Many new riders are concerned about using their front brake," said Eric Owens, who led the workshop on braking. "They are afraid that they might go over the handlebars. This leads them to rely on the rear brake—which has only 30% of the braking power.

Our session on braking includes instruction on how to use both the front and rear brakes at the same time, down-shifting when necessary. It's also very important to be at almost a complete stop before putting your left foot on the ground. If you put your foot down while the bike is going too fast, you run a high risk of an accident."

The workshop on shifting

Photo by Jean Brunelle

A helmet with face guard, plus protective clothing, are musts for safe motorcycle riding.

gears emphasizied the coordination needed in order to shift without losing control of the motorcycle. Shifting gears requires control of the clutch, throttle and gear shift lever.

Maintenance was a popular workshop at the Rodeo. "Making sure your motorcycle is in top condition is an important part of safe riding," says workshop leader George McCall. "A mechanic should inspect the bike at regular intervals," says McCall. "But a rider should be alert for signs of trouble. Owners should also know how to adjust and clean certain parts, and make minor repairs. A safe machine is

a well-maintained machine."

The most important piece of protective gear a rider can wear is a helmet. The workshop on this topic stressed the necessity of wearing a secure, shatter-proof helmet which includes eye protection. "In addition," states workshop leader Katie Kelly, "riders should also wear leather gloves, strong, over-the-ankle boots, and long-sleeved jackets and pants. Leather clothing is preferred by most experienced drivers. It offers maximum protection in the event of a spill."

Participants in the rodeo each received a certificate for taking part.

How To Study

Practice Using Your Newspaper

Find two fairly long articles which interest you. For each one, do the following:

1. Underline main ideas and important details as you read.

2. Make an outline, or study guide, of this article using information you underlined.

3. Think of two questions or comments about this subject which you might contribute to a classroom discussion.

Main Idea _____

_____

    Detail _____

_____

Main Idea _____

_____

    Detail _____

_____

Main Idea _____

_____

    Detail _____

_____

Question _____

_____

Comment _____

_____

Now Try Your Newspower

Follow a continuing story in your newspaper for one week. This may be continuing news of a case in court, an election, a tragedy, a battle in Congress, etc.

- Cut out an article about the story each day.

- Mark the most important ideas and details.

- Write down questions and comments.

- Hold a class discussion about the subject, using your notes as a guide.

Students tend to think of tests as surprises. Who knows what might be on them? Actually, most tests are predictable. Tests are used to check your knowledge of the most important facts, ideas, and procedures you have studied. If you have done a good job of tracking these things in your marking and note-taking, you have a handy reference of everything you can be asked.

Your first job in preparing for a test, then, is to review all you have done in your studying. Get a good general picture of all the information you can be questioned about. Then prepare for the test by asking yourself questions the teacher is likely to ask. Find the answers to your questions in your notes or your textbook. When you come to take the test, you will be surprised at how many of the questions you have already asked–and answered–in your studying.

Because there are basically two kinds of tests–short answer and long answer (essay)–try to find out from your teacher in advance the kind of test you will be taking. You study for them in slightly different ways.

Short-Answer Questions

Short-answer questions come in many forms. You've probably met all of them at some point in your school career. They include true-false, matching, multiple-choice, filling in blanks, and sentence completion.

Another name for these kinds of questions is objective questions. They check your knowledge of facts, details, and main ideas.

To prepare for objective tests, you should study definitions, main ideas, dates, names of persons, places and things–in short, the who, what, where, and when types of information. When you prepare for short-answer tests, ask yourself questions like these:

<u>Who</u> won the Battle of Little Big Horn?

<u>What</u> is the definition of a line segment?

<u>Where</u> can you find the pulse point on the neck?

<u>When</u> did man set foot on the moon?

Essay Questions

The other major kind of test question is called the essay question. This kind of question asks you to explain the whys and hows of things. They ask for causes, results, and relationships. Here are some examples of essay questions:

• Why couldn't the Native Americans and the white settlers share the western plains peacefully?

• Describe a process for combining hydrogen and oxygen to make water.

• Explain how the development of the atomic bomb changed the course of history.

Questions like these test your understanding of a subject. Essay questions are more challenging to answer than objective questions. You can't memorize the answers to them. Instead, they require you to think and then answer in complete sentences.

Preparing for Tests

Essay Questions *(cont.)*

To prepare for them you must 1) know your facts, and 2) look for cause-and-effect relationships.

1. **Know Your Facts.** These are the same who, what, where, and when facts you study for short answer questions. You will use these to "prove" your answer.

2. **Look for Cause-and-Effect Relationships.** A cause-and-effect relationship means that one thing causes another thing to happen. For instance, the transcontinental railroad caused a faster westward expansion of the United States. Suppose an essay question asked, "What was the significance of the transcontinental railroad?" To answer, you would point out this cause-and-effect relationship. You would back up your answer with facts to prove your point:

   • The railroad brought new settlers.

   • The railroad opened up new land.

   • The railroad allowed shipment of farm products to the east.

Reviewing for Tests

There are four resources you should use when reviewing for a test: your textbook, classroom handouts, your notes, and any quizzes you have taken.

1. **Review Your Textbook.** This is your main resource when studying for a test. But don't read it word for word. You have already done that once. Instead, reread chapter introductions, headings, sub-headings, and anything in bold type or otherwise set apart. Also look at pictures, picture captions, charts, and graphs. If you marked your text or jotted down main ideas and details, as suggested in Lesson 2, now is the time to review them.

2. **Review Any Handouts.** Many teachers pass out extra sheets of information during the course. Be sure to review such classroom handouts. One or more questions on a test is sure to come from them.

3. **Review Class Notes.** Review any notes that you took in class. What points did your teacher bring up in class? What topics were covered? These are sure to be on the test.

4. **Review Previous Quizzes.** Finally, save all quizzes you have taken during the course. Correct any answers that were marked wrong. Review the information that the quizzes contained. Often, each quiz turns out to be part of the final test.

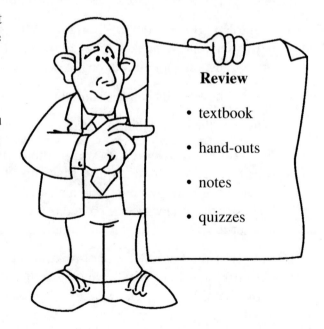

Write Your Own Test!

The single most important thing you can do to prepare for a test is to write a test of your own. To do this, of course, you have to know your subject. You have to do your reading. You have to review all of the information, and you have to decide what's important and what isn't. So you see, just the process of writing your own test helps you to learn the material.

Preparing for Tests

Write Your Own Test! *(cont.)*

It's not hard to write your own test. And it's a great learning experience. Here's how to go about it:

1. **Ask Your Teacher about the Upcoming Test**. Some things you want to find out are:

   - What will the test cover?

   - What kind of questions will be asked—objective or essay questions?

   Don't be afraid to ask for information. It shows you are interested in preparing for the test. The worst that can happen is your teacher will say no.

2. **Divide Your Test Material into Sections**. Now that you know what the test will cover, divide it into sections. For instance, if your test covers four chapters, divide your test into four sections, one for each chapter. If your test will cover the Civil War, divide your test into beginning, middle and end of the Civil War. The point is to make sure you write test questions that cover the whole subject you will be tested on.

3. **Make Up Short-Answer Questions** for everything in bold type, and for every chapter and section heading in your textbook. Important words are usually printed in darker type the first time they are used. Write a question checking your knowledge of this word. If a section in your history book is titled "The Battle of Bull Run," write one or two test questions about the dates and outcome of this battle.

   Ask your questions so they can be answered in just a few words. It doesn't matter if your test has multiple-choice questions, fill-ins, matching questions, true-false questions, or some of each. The facts will fit into any form easily.

4. **Make Up One Essay Question for Each Section**. Think: what is the single most important point in this section? What is mentioned over and over again? When you have identified this, write an essay question about it that begins with the words "Why . . ." or "Explain . . ."

   Explain how plants convert sunlight into energy.

   Why was the theory that the earth moves around the sun hotly debated in the early 17th century?

5. **For Math and Science**, ask yourself to define special terms you have learned. Make up problems or redo problems you have had for homework. Review special procedures your teacher has said are important to know.

6. **Finally, Take Your Own Test!** Answer the objective questions, even if you know that you know them. Write the answers to your essay questions.

   For math and science, rework problems. Write out formulas and procedures.

   By the time you finish this exercise, you'll feel you know your subject inside out.

Take Your own Test!

Preparing for Tests

Exercise C

The following article is divided into four sections. Read the story and then write your own test questions, as directed on the next page.

Destination: Marble Point

MCMURDO SOUND, ANTARCTICA–It's spring in Antarctica, where a day can last six months and the temperature can plunge to 80 below zero in winter. Nothing grows except cracks in the ice. Yet this frozen continent is home to a unique band of sailors. Their ships are bulldozers, and they sail a frozen sea. Their job is to deliver supplies to Marble Point, a remote outpost some 140 dangerous miles away.

A bulldozer revs its engines and tugs on its two flatbed trailer sleds. Another dozer pulls two more sleds–one loaded with fuel, and the other rigged with a box-like sleeping shelter. Navyman Skip Carroll scans the horizon. His job is to pick a safe route for the convoy. There is no map. There are no roads. There are no signs pointing the way. Their only guides are experience and keen eyes. "And my sixth sense!" jokes Carroll.

A convoy scout checks a crevice in the ice.

A Harsh Environment

"We're traveling over water with an average depth of a thousand feet below the ice," explains Carroll, 24. "The risks of falling through aren't really that great. The real risk is getting socked in by the weather."

In a matter of hours, Antarctic's weather can change from clear and sunny to a raging blizzard–a white-out. When that happens, the convoy calls a halt and the sailors gather in their make-shift shelter. It's got a heater, food, portable cookstove, and bunk beds. And it's home, home on the ice.

The trip can take its toll on a person. "Fatigue is a real problem for the drivers," says Jake Ware of Iowa. "We sit perched in that dozer for hours on end, staring hard at not much at all. The mind can begin to play tricks on a guy. When you see something that isn't there, you know it's time to stop and rest."

How Do You Check a Crack? Very Carefully!

But it's never boring. Every crack in the ice is a potential danger, and has to be checked out. Up ahead, Skip Carroll gets on his hands and knees to check out an 8-inch crack. He looks for signs of age and frost inside the split. He walks its length to see if it is pulling apart. Finally, he signals back to the convoy to drive around it.

"Sometimes we unhook sleds and cross with the dozer first," explains Ware. "Then, once the dozer is over safely, we hook the sleds to a winch cable and bring them across."

Change Comes to Antarctica

This run, the convoy is bringing prefab buildings to Marble Point. The shipment will make Marble Point a permanent working U.S. Facility. Scientific research can go on year-round. Seismic studies can provide insights into earthquakes. Sampling the air can reveal pollution problems. Projects like these can benefit the world as a whole. Marble Point may never be a boom town, but its contributions will far outweigh its size.

Preparing for Tests

Exercise C *(cont.)*

1. Reread the first paragraph of the article. The job of the sailors at McMurdo Sound is stated in the last sentence. Write a short-answer question based on this information.

_____

_____

_____

_____

2. Reread the section titled *A Harsh Environment*. Choose the most important fact contained in each paragraph. Then write a short-answer question for each paragraph.

Paragraph 1 _____

_____

_____

Paragraph 2 _____

_____

_____

Paragraph 3 _____

_____

_____

3. Reread the section titled *How Do You Check a Crack*? Again, choose an important fact. Then write a question based on this fact.

_____

_____

_____

4. Reread the section titled *Change Comes to Antarctica*. Think about what you read. Then write an essay question asking about the effects of a permanent research station at Marble Point.

_____

_____

_____

Preparing for Tests

Practice Using Your Newspaper

Choose one long article that interests you in your newspaper. Read the whole article. Divide it into three or four sections. Write two short-answer test questions for each section. Save the test you have written and the article. You will be using them at the end of Lesson 4. When you are finished, try this same exercise using a chapter or a section from one of your textbooks.

Name of Article _____

Section 1

1. _____

_____

2. _____

_____

Section 2

3. _____

_____

4. _____

_____

Section 3

5. _____

_____

6. _____

_____

Section 4

7. _____

_____

8. _____

_____

Now Try Your Newspower

Essay questions give students the most trouble on tests. Practice answering essay questions by completing the following activity. Choose any article in your newspaper that deals with a serious problem. Read it carefully. Answer this essay-type question: How might what you have read change your life, or change someone else's life, or change your town? Use examples and facts from the article to support your answer.

Taking Tests

Most people feel at least a little anxious when they take a test. However, there are certain things you can do, both before and during the test, that can make the experience easier for you.

Get Off to a Good Start

On the day of your test, get up in time to enjoy a good breakfast. Think of it as brain food. The last thing you want to cope with is mid-morning hunger slump.

Don't panic. If you have prepared well, you will be okay. If you are tense or frightened, take a deep breath, let it out and tell yourself to relax. Remember, although you would like to do well, no test is the end of the world.

Plan Your Strategy

When you have received your test, look it over. Spend a minute or two planning your strategy. If there are several essay questions at the end, don't spend too much time on the short-answer part of the test. Plan your time. Then, plunge ahead!

Short-Answer Questions

Go through and answer those short-answer questions you are sure of first. Next, answer the questions you are fairly sure of. Leave the hardest questions until the end. Remember, don't spend a lot of time on one difficult question and ignore other questions which you may get right.

A good rule of thumb is not to leave blank answers. If you're not sure of an answer, guess at one–unless your teacher says you will be penalized for guessing. Spend any leftover time reviewing what you have written. But don't change any answers unless you are positive, your first guess is often the best guess.

Essay Questions

Essay questions call for detailed written answers. This type of question will take the most time and it is important not to waste steps.

To begin with, read the entire question carefully and decide exactly what is being asked for. Watch for key words such as "Give three reasons. . ." "Explain the ways. . ." "Describe the main character . . ." "Compare . . ." For example, if a question asks you to explain the issues which led to the Civil War, don't ramble on about details of specific battles. Also, try to give facts and examples that support, or prove, the statements you make.

Begin by making a very brief outline for yourself. Do this right on the test paper if there is room, or on a separate piece of paper. Don't worry about making a formal outline, but do make a list of the facts and ideas you want to include in your answer. Number them in the order in which you want to talk about them. Then cross each item off your outline as you include it in your answer.

If you have enough time, write a rough answer first and then revise it to make it better on your test paper.

Taking Tests

Math and Science Problems

If there is a formula or a set procedure to follow, write this down on your test paper. Keep referring to it. Work carefully and check your work after each step. Watch for steps left out.

Finally, think about your answer. Does it sound reasonable? Estimate an answer in your head, using rounded-off numbers. Check signs–did you add instead of subtract? multiply instead of divide? Make sure you show on your test paper the different procedures you have tried with the math or science problem. Teachers will often give partial credit for good tries.

Review Your Work

When you're finished, use any leftover time for review. Make small corrections in spelling and punctuation. These changes will make your paper easier to read for your teacher. They will also improve your grade.

If you think of additional information which might improve an answer, add it. But don't do a major rewrite in the last couple of minutes.

If you are having difficulty, don't throw in the towel. Keep working on your paper as long as you can. Something will come to you if you keep thinking and jotting down thoughts as they occur. Sometimes even a stray thought will trigger a good answer.

A Test-Taking Checklist

Read each of the questions below carefully and answer with a Yes or No. No answers are areas in which you need to improve. Review this checklist well in advance of any test you take.

	Yes	No
1. Do you study and review regularly all through the term, not just before tests?		
2. Are your assignments and notes up to date?		
3. Do you plan a review schedule a week or two before tests?		
4. Have you prepared review outlines to help you study?		
5. Do you ask your teacher's advice on how and what to prepare for on an upcoming test?		
6. Do you get enough sleep the night before a test?		
7. Do you eat a good breakfast the day of the test?		
8. Do you read and follow directions carefully?		
9. Do you answer easier questions first, and then go back to the more difficult ones?		
10. Do you budget your time?		
11. Do you make outlines for essay questions?		
12. Do you write down formulas and procedures?		

Taking Tests

Exercise D

Read the following feature story. Then complete the exercise on page 25.

Video Center Offers Training

GAYLE, MD—The Center for Video Studies is offering a course on how to use video equipment. Director Susan Mariac will teach the "hands-on" classes. The topics to be covered include using a video camera, the portapak deck, and microphones. At the end of the six-week course, each student will produce an original video tape.

"One of the most important rules about using a video camera," says Ms. Mariac, "is to keep the viewer in mind. Too many beginners try a lot of tricks and gimmicks with the camera. They zoom in and out on an image so quickly that it leaves the viewer dizzy. Or, they shoot an object that is too far away and the screen then looks empty. Another common mistake is to pan a scene so quickly that the viewer can't get a sense of what is going on."

A good general rule is to divide the screen mentally into three parts: lower, middle and upper. Then make sure that your shot has something different in each third of the screen. A shot of a sailboat, for instance, should show the sea in the bottom third of the picture, the boat in the middle, and the sky in the upper third.

The portapak deck looks much like a tape recorder. The video-tape is placed in the deck. Then the camera is attached to the control panel on the deck.

The deck is powered by either electrical current or battery power. A professional camera technician, perhaps working for a TV station, knows the

Shooting a live news story.

importance of having a fully charged battery in the deck at all times. "No power, no picture," smiles Ms. Mariac, who says she's learned this lesson the hard way.

Ms. Mariac says that learning to handle microphones can be the most difficult part of working with video equipment. "People get so concerned with the picture that they forget the sound track needs attention too."

Finally, you have to learn how to make all this equipment tell a story or provide information. This skill has nothing to do with operating the equipment.

Take a wedding, for instance. "Many couples today," says Ms. Mariac, "want a videotape of their wedding. If they hire me to do that, I've got to plan what to shoot, and when to shoot it. I want to get the ceremony, of course. But I don't want to be off interviewing guests when the bride cuts the cake." This skill requires setting goals and planning how you will achieve them.

Producing videos is a great introduction to movie making, concludes Ms. Mariac. All future movie moguls are invited to sign up for her course.

Taking Tests

Exercise D (cont.)

Imagine you are planning to make a 20-minute video about good study habits. Make a four-part plan (five minutes each) that outlines what your actors or actresses will say, and what scenes your camera will record. Review Lessons 1 through 4 for information to use. Part I is done for you as an example.

Part I: Getting Organized

Scene 1: Student sprawled on bed, yawning, trying to study.

Audio: Narrator describes poor study habits shown in picture.

Scene 2: Student seated at properly equipped desk or study area.

Audio: Narrator describes what makes a good study place, and how to manage study time.

Part II: How to Study

Scene 1:_____

_____

Audio: _____

Scene 2:_____

_____

Audio: _____

Part III: Preparing for Tests

Scene 1:_____

_____

Audio: _____

Scene 2:_____

_____

Audio: _____

Part IV: Taking Tests

Scene 1:_____

_____

Audio: _____

Scene 2:_____

_____

Audio: _____

Taking Tests

Practice Using Your Newspaper

1. Take the newspaper article and the test you wrote at the end of Lesson 3.

2. Exchange these with another student who used a different article.

3. Read the article carefully and then take the test.

4. Exchange tests when you have both finished, and correct each other's answers.

Now Try Your Newspower

Suppose you are told this: "One week from today you will be tested on the sports section of today's newspaper."

Draw up a study schedule for the coming week that you could use to prepare for such a test. You might want to go about it in the following way:

1. Divide your study outline into sections, one for each day of the week.

2. Go through the sports section of your newspaper and divide it into sections also.

3. For each section of your outline, show the following:

   a) What you will study that day.

   b) How much time you will spend on it.

   c) Your study goal for that day.

4. Be sure to include review time in your schedule.

Mon.	Tue.	Wed.

Thurs.	Fri.	Sat./Sun.

Chapter 2: Vocabulary and Context

Introduction

> *"O frabjous day! Calooh! Callay!"*

Three of these five words make no sense at all. They were made up, in fact, by Lewis Carroll for his famous nonsense poem, "Jabberwocky." So what is a reader to make of them? Very little, if you only read that one line of the poem. But add the next line and see what you can figure out about the words frabjous, callooh, and callay:

> *"O frabjous day! Calooh! Callay!"*
> *He chortled in his joy.*

The one word you can be sure of in these two lines is the word joy. Someone is joyful. And that alone is enough to tell you that frabjous, callooh, callay, and chortle all suggest happiness. Thus you could "translate" these two lines to read this:

> *"O happy day! Hurrah! Hooray!"*
> *He chuckled in his joy.*

That's what is meant by *vocabulary in context*. Context refers to the surrounding words, sentences, and paragraphs. They contain valuable clues that can help you understand new words without looking them up in the dictionary. There's no substitute for a dictionary, of course. But you don't always need to know the exact meaning of every word. Sometimes you just need to know "the gist of it." This can often be found in the tone of the passage, from the subject matter, or from synonyms and explanations the writer uses.

These are all *context clues* that help you to decipher new words from the way they are used–from their context, in other words. The skills you learn in the next five lessons will help you to deal with new words wherever you meet them–in newspapers, in magazines, in textbooks, in stories, and even in the course of everyday conversation.

Using Tone To Understand New Words

When Miss Piggy coos, "Oh, Kermit, you're so–so *trés formidable!*" You don't need to know French to understand that she's paying him a compliment. You can tell by the tone of her voice that she finds him "very enchanting!"

You can "hear" tone in your reading as clearly as you can hear a person's tone of voice. Tone reveals feelings. And if you've ever felt "moved" by something you've read, then you have sensed its tone.

This arms you with a valuable clue to understanding new words. If you meet an unfamiliar word, its meaning may be linked to the tone. Watch how it works in the following news article. Listen for its tone. (Hint: How does the President feel?) Then decide what this tells you about the meaning of the underlined word in the last sentence.

Civilian Airline Shot Down

WASHINGTON—White House officials say they are "extremely distressed" over the downing of an airliner filled with vacationing tourists. The plane apparently strayed off course and was shot down over hostile territory. Says the President, "We are outraged over this <u>heinous</u> action."

The President says he is "outraged" by the shooting down of the airliner. This is how he feels, so this is the tone of his remark. Therefore a *heinous* action must be something terrible–something that makes you feel outraged. And that, as it turns out, is what the word *heinous* means–something extremely wicked.

Tone won't help you to define a new word, of course. But it does point you in the right direction. See how the tone of this next story narrows down the meaning of the word *fervor*.

Mother Pleads for Organ Transplant Center

WASHINGTON—A dedicated mother asked Congress to fund a central clearinghouse to match up organ donors with transplant patients. "The Tin Man went to the Wizard of Oz in search of a heart," said Mrs. DeGrenier of Queens, New York. "But there is no Emerald City for the thousands of patients, young and old, who will die unless they get a new heart, or a new liver, or a new kidney. But **you** can help," she said with a <u>fervor</u> that seemed to come from the heart. Mrs. DeGrenier's three-year old daughter died last year while awaiting a new kidney.

The tone of this mother's speech is very emotional and full of feeling. So when you come to the word fervor, you know that it must describe this same kind of deep emotion. She spoke "with a fervor that seemed to come from the heart." She didn't speak calmly, or reluctantly–she spoke movingly and with genuine feeling. This is the definition of fervor, and it matches the tone of the mother's remarks.

Using Tone To Understand New Words

Keep in mind that there may be more than one tone in the same article. Tone changes as feelings change. So when you use tone to help you understand a new word, make sure you identify the tone at that point.

Here's a story with three different tones. See if you can spot the different tones by the way your feelings change. What do they tell you about the meaning of the underlined words?

Amusement Park Tragedy

Eyewitness describes ordeal

YORK SPRING—"I really didn't want to go on it," say Kelly Cameron recalling the ill-fated Red Baron ride at the York Springs amusement park. "Just watching the ride made me feel uneasy. As I gave the attendant my ticket, I felt this strange tightness in my chest—like I couldn't breathe. I had a sudden <u>presentiment</u> of danger.

"As our airplane gained speed, I suddenly gripped my friend's hand. Then it happened. The cable attached to the nose of our plane just—let go. Jerry and I pitched forward against the safety bar. The next moment we were dangling by the tail. Then everyone started slamming into each other. It was like the bumper cars—50 feet up. I heard screams and realized some of them were mine. It was sheer <u>bedlam</u>.

"Finally the fire department came with cherry-picker cranes to pluck us out. 'Is this part of the ride?' Jerry asked them. 'Sure—and I'm the Red Baron!' *quipped* our rescuer. He looked more like an angel to me. That's one ride that was as unforgettable as they promised!"

Each paragraph of this story has a different tone. The first paragraph has a fearful tone. Kelly had the feeling that something bad was going to happen. She gives us that feeling too. So when we come to the word presentiment—"I had a sudden presentiment of danger"—the tone suggests that a presentiment is something like a warning.

In the second paragraph the tone grows more dramatic. The riders are crashing into each other. People are screaming. We share Kelly's feelings of frantic terror, and conclude that bedlam must mean a place of terrified confusion.

In the last paragraph the tone is more relaxed. The crisis is over, and people sound relieved. "Is this part of the ride?" Jerry jokes. "Sure–and I'm the Red Baron!" quips their rescuer. From the tone of this scene you can tell that "to quip" probably means to make a joking remark. It's a light-hearted word that matches the light-hearted tone of this passage.

Using tone to understand new words works best when the story or article expresses a strong emotion. But tone is not the only kind of context clue. Lesson 2 will explain how ideas and topics also help identify a strange word.

Using Tone to Understand New Words

Exercise A

Read the feature article carefully and answer the questions that follow.

From Hoes to Tractors – and Back Again

Part 1

The 1960's were a time of great hope for underdeveloped countries. The "Green Revolution" in agriculture had arrived. Huge tractors enabled farmers in Asia and Africa to till more land. Modern irrigation systems brought water to the desert. Hybrid strains of rice, corn and wheat produced "super crops" that were hardier and more productive. Chemical fertilizers protected the new varieties from insect damage and disease.

The Green Revolution extended to fishing as well. Such ancient fishing methods as spears and nets were being replaced by modern trawlers equipped with radar, sonar and other high-tech fishing equipment.

As world food production soared, experts made *sanguine* predictions. "We will feed not only ourselves, but our neighbors," proclaimed one African leader.

Part 2

And then came the oil embargoes of the 1970's, and the fuel shortages which followed. Suddenly the price of gasoline skyrocketed. Giant farm machines sat idle in the fields, their fuel tanks empty. The cost of chemical fertilizers-petrochemical fertilizers made from petroleum-shot up too. Without them, the miracle crops fell prey to age-old plagues of insects and disease. A decade-long drought in parts of Africa further decimated the Green Revolution. The result: wide-

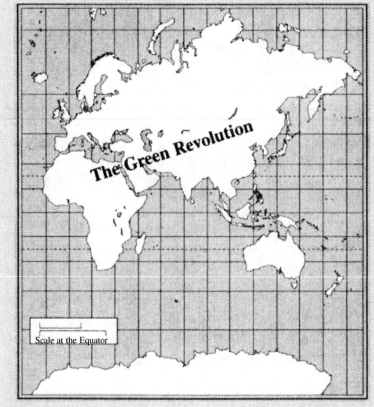

The Green Revolution

Scale at the Equator

spread starvation and human misery on a massive scale. Refugees from drought-stricken areas embarked on a desperate journey for food. One man told how he and his family hiked for more than a week to get to Zimbabwe from Tete. "There is nothing there," he said of his home territory. "We were walking through villages of death." *Emaciated*, frail and *ravaged* by hunger, many perished.

Lately, however, things have been looking up. Farming is on the upswing again. But this time it is farming on a much smaller scale.

Part 3

Farmers are returning to such traditional crops as rice, cassava, and couscous. And they are planting them by hand, like their ancestors have done for centuries. Such methods can be back-breaking and tedious. But they're performed by human power and animal power. No gasoline required.

It is an *auspicious* trend, and national leaders feel encouraged. "It is not a cure-all," said one African leader recently. "And it will not feed thousands. But it can be the salvation of a small village or community."

Using Tone To Understand New Words

Exercise A *(cont.)*

After reading the article on page 30, complete the following exercise.

Part 1

1. Part 1 describes the "Green Revolution" and the changes it brought to farming and fishing. The tone of this section makes you feel

    ( ) a. angry   ( ) c. sad

    ( ) b. hopeful   ( ) d. guilty

2. From the tone of Part 1, you can guess that a "sanguine prediction" is probably

    ( ) a. hopeful or confident   ( ) c. uncertain or doubtful

    ( ) b. bad news   ( ) d. a good guess

Part 2

3. In Part 2, the tone of this article becomes

    ( ) a. comical and upbeat   ( ) c. angry

    ( ) b. matter-of-fact   ( ) d. troubled and tragic

4. What does the tone tell you about words like emaciated and ravaged?

    ( ) a. They probably describe a very bad   ( ) c. They describe a situation that
          situation.   is getting better.

    ( ) b. They have something to do with Africa.   ( ) d. They describe ragged and
                                                             dirty clothing.

Part 3

5. In Part 3 the tone changes once again. This time it reflects a feeling of

    ( ) a. despair   ( ) c. new hope

    ( ) b. regret   ( ) d. frustration

6. The return to traditional farming, says the writer, is "an auspicious trend." The tone of this part of the story is a clue that an auspicious trend is

    ( ) a. a trend towards something better   ( ) c. a last resort

    ( ) b. a move in the wrong direction   ( ) d. yet another failure

Optional Exercise

Guess at the meaning of the following words which also appear in the article you have just read. Then find the words in a dictionary to see how close you came to the correct meaning.

trawler	petrochemical	decade
decimated	massive	traditional
tedious	salvation	

Using Tone To Understand New Words

Practice Using Your Newspaper

People write letters to the editor because they feel strongly about something. You can tell how they feel by the tone of their letter.

Read two letters to the editor. For each one:

1. Find the words that help you to feel this letter's tone. Write them down.
2. Find words in the letters whose meanings you are not sure of. Write them down.
3. Guess at the words' meanings from the tone of the letter.
4. Check your guesses by looking up the words in a dictionary.

Letter #1

1. Words that help create the letter's tone _____

   _____

2. Words whose meanings you are not sure of _____

   _____

3. What you think the words mean _____

   _____

   _____

4. What the dictionary says _____

   _____

   _____

   _____

Letter #2

1. Words that help create the letter's tone _____

   _____

2. Words whose meaning you are not sure _____

   _____

3. What you think the words mean _____

   _____

   _____

4. What the dictionary says _____

   _____

   _____

   _____

Using Tone To Understand New Words

Now Try Your Newspower

Make a collection of expressions and sentences that do a good job of carrying a feeling—ones that have a clear tone, in other words. Here's how:

- Each day, find at least two sentences or expressions in your newspaper that carry feelings.

- Copy the expressions in the boxes below.

- Write a short sentence that tells what kind of tone each expression carries.

- If there are words you do not understand, first guess at the meaning of the word, and then look up the meaning in a dictionary. Write the meaning of these new words on your cards.

- Some examples:

    It's a horrible situation. (Tone is anger or disgust.)

    The growing plight of homeless. (Tone is pitying. The word plight means a sad condition or situation.)

    Let's stop being wishy-washy people. (Tone is teaching or pleading. The expression wishy-washy means weak)

- Keep adding to your card collection for two weeks, or as long as your teacher wants you to.

Expression: _____ _____ _____ **Tone:** _____ _____ _____	**Expression:** _____ _____ _____ **Tone:** _____ _____ _____
Expression: _____ _____ _____ **Tone:** _____ _____ _____	**Expression:** _____ _____ _____ **Tone:** _____ _____ _____

Using the Subject as a Context Clue

The words you read in a story, article, or chapter all have something to do with the main subject or ideas being discussed. This is important to remember. Because if you can identify the subject, this can provide a clue to the meaning of unfamiliar words.

Watch how it works in this next article. Read the article and decide what the story is about. This is the subject. Then take a second look at the underlined words. How does knowing the subject help you with the meanings of words?

Police Investigate Mysterious Death

THORNHILL—Police say they are looking into the death of the university's star quarterback, who passed out during half-time Saturday. The young man was rushed by ambulance to Mercy Hospital where he died a short time later.

The *coroner* will do an *autopsy* on the body to determine the cause of death. If evidence of foul play is found, then an *inquest* will be held. Detective Peter O' Malley said, "Young men do not pass away on the playing field without a reason. We intend to find out what that reason is."

The *bereaved* family appeared very *distraught* and would not talk to reporters.

This article is about the mysterious death of a football player. That is the subject. And all of the information in the article is related to this death. So there's a good chance that any unfamiliar words will also have something to do with death, especially an unexplained death.

Start with the second paragraph: "The *coroner* will do an *autopsy* on the body to determine the cause of death." It sounds like a coroner is someone, probably a doctor, who looks into unexplained deaths. An autopsy must be a kind of examination done after death.

The story goes on to say that, "If evidence of foul play is found, then an *inquest* will be held." An inquest seems to be a formal sort of investigation of a suspicious death.

The last paragraph says, "The *bereaved* family appeared very *distraught*." Since this family just lost a son and brother, the word "bereaved" must refer to anyone who has lost a close friend or relative. And since anyone who is bereaved is likely to be very upset, "distraught" probably means extremely upset.

None of these meanings is the full meaning, or even the exact meaning. But they are all close enough to allow you to understand what you are reading. And that is the point of using context clues to understand new words.

Look for the main idea in Exercise B and see what it tells you about any new words you meet.

Using the Subject as a Context Clue

Exercise B

Read the newspaper article carefully and answer the questions on page 36.

Bees Are Their Business

Part 1

WEMBLEY—Beekeepers Jason and Sarah Singly have made a business out of *apiculture*. The Singlys keep about 40 hives in the *apiary* in their backyard. Needless to say, the family cooks with honey, spreads it on their toast, and sweetens their coffee and tea with it. "I don't serve toasted honeybees as a snack," says Sarah with a smile. "But they do in some parts of the world."

Apiculture represents an important part of the family income. "We sell honey in both liquid and comb form at farm stands and health food stores," says Sarah. "Plus I make my own beeswax candles which are sold in craft shops." But these are just the by-products of apiculture.

Part 2

The real business of bees, of course, is agriculture. Called "the angels of agriculture," bees pollinate apple orchards and other flowering crops so blossoms develop into fruit. During the early spring, Jason rents the hives to orchard owners for a week to ten days to ensure proper *pollination*.

"Misshaped apples," notes Sarah, "are often caused by inadequate pollination."

"Do you ever get stung?" I asked.

"All the time," said Jason with a grin and a shrug. "See, there's one on my arm right now." As we watched a bee vigorously pumped *venom* into his forearm. The stinger, actually a pair of sliding saw-toothed knives, tends to catch in the skin of large victims such as ourselves. This tears the stinger from the bee's

Protective clothing is a must for beekeepers.   Photo by Stan Sherer

Part 3

abdomen, killing her. "Hurts her more than it does me!" laughed Jason.

Bee stings are no laughing matter, however, to people who are allergic to them. Hymenopterism can send its victims into shock, and even cause death. But as for those so-called "killer bees" of the horror movies, they're strictly an invention of Hollywood script writers, claims Jason. "All told, we pose a far greater threat to honeybees than they do to us."

The honeybee, in fact, has many enemies. In a natural setting, *predators* such as badgers, rodents, shrews, and honey-loving bears regularly raid the hives. Some birds such as woodpeckers and fly-catchers are fond of bees, honey, and beeswax. So is a species of wasps called "bee wolves," which feed honeybees to their young.

Part 4

But the greatest danger of all comes from chemical *pesticides* some farmers spray on their crops. "I don't know of any pesticide that does not harm bees," states Jason. "It's ironic- farmers spray pesticides on their crops to help them grow, and at the same time they kill the bees which perform the vital chore of pollination."

The Singlys frequently display a working beehive at schools and libraries in the area.

Using the Subject as a Context Clue

Exercise B *(cont.)*

Circle the correct choice.

Part 1

1. Re-read Part 1 of the article. The subject of this section is

   a. beekeeping as a business.

   b. uses of honey.

   c. bees throughout history.

   d. how to construct a hive.

2. The subject of this section is a clue to the meanings of the words apiculture and apiary. These words probably have something to do with

   a. natural sweeteners.

   b. making beeswax candles.

   c. raising bees.

   d. treating bee stings.

Part 2

3. The subject of Part 2 deals with bees and

   a. big business.

   b. flower gardens.

   c. angels.

   d. agriculture.

4. The subject of this section tells you that the term pollination refers to

   a. a way in which bees aid agriculture.

   b. a certain species of honeybee.

   c. a new variety of apple.

   d. a stage of growth in young bees.

Part 3

5. Part 3 of the article is mainly about

   a. common allergies.

   b. bee stings.

   c. Hollywood horror movies.

   d. killer bees.

6. This part tells you that hymenopterism, a condition which can send its victims into shock and even cause death, is caused by

   a. springtime allergies.

   b. killer bees.

   c. bee stings.

   d. pollination.

Part 4

7. The last part of the article deals with

   a. chemicals used in farming.

   b. bee wolves.

   c. enemies of bees.

   d. the Singly's display at the county fair.

8. The subject of Part 4 is a clue that pesticides and predators are both

   a. harmful to bees.

   b. used by farmers to help crops grow.

   c. endangered species.

   d. fond of honey.

Using the Subject as a Context Clue

Practice Using Your Newspaper

Choose two rather long articles in the newspaper that interest you. For each article, do the following:

1. Read the article and decide what it is about. This is its subject. Write this on the line provided.
2. Find three words whose meanings you are unsure of. Write them in the spaces below.
3. Think about how each word might relate to the subject of the article. Then try to decide what each word means. Write your definition on the lines provided. If you can't think of a definition, tell how you think the word is related to the subject.
4. Check your definitions using a dictionary. Write the dictionary definition in the space provided.

Article 1

Subject: _____

Word #1: _____ Your definition: _____

Dictionary definition: _____

Word #2: _____ Your definition: _____

Dictionary definition: _____

_____

Word #3: _____ Your definition: _____

Dictionary definition: _____

_____

Article 2

Subject: _____

Word #1: _____ Your definition: _____

Dictionary definition: _____

_____

Word #2: _____ Your definition: _____

Dictionary definition: _____

_____

Word #3: _____ Your definition: _____

Dictionary definition: _____

_____

Using the Subject as a Context Clue

Now Try Your Newspower

Find the most difficult word you can in your newspaper. Save the newspaper article which contains the word. Other people in your class, or in your family, should do the same thing. Then, do the following:

1. Each person shows his or her word to all the others.

2. Read the article aloud that contains the word.

3. Ask each person to give an opinion about how the word is related to the subject of the article.

4. Each person takes a turn guessing at the meaning of the word.

5. Look up the word in a dictionary and announce the dictionary's definition.

   Optional question: If the dictionary gives more than one definition for a word, how does the subject of the article help you select the definition you want?

Word: _____

How it is related to the subject of the article: _____

_____

_____

_____

_____

My guess of the definition: _____

_____

_____

_____

_____

The dictionary's definition: _____

_____

_____

_____

_____

Using Synonyms and Explanations as Context Clues

Sharp readers find even more context clues to help them understand new words.

Synonyms often help. Synonyms (sin-o-nims) are different words that have nearly the same meaning, as in this sentence: *"It was a hot, sultry day."*

The way they are used here, "hot" and "sultry" mean much the same thing. And you can guess from the first what the second word means. As a rule of thumb, when two adjectives are used to describe the same thing, they often have similar or related meanings.

Another kind of context clue consists of *explanations* provided by the author. Authors want readers to understand what they write. When they use a word that readers may not be familiar with, they often explain it. This is especially true for words that belong to a *special vocabulary*. A special vocabulary means any group of words that is used mainly by one group of people. Doctors, for instance, have a special vocabulary. It includes words like arteriosclerosis, hypertension, thrombosis, and so on. The average person may not know these words. They don't have to, because they're not doctors. So when authors use one of these words, they often explain it for readers in context.

Watch how the term "cardiopulmonary resuscitation" is explained in the context of this next article:

Teen Saves Life at Reunion

ORANGE—Chris Walker knew just what to do when his aunt, Wilma Walker, collapsed of a heart attack at the Walker family reunion Sunday. The 16-year old immediately began cardiopulmonary resuscitation (CPR) to circulate blood and provide oxygen until heart and lung function could be restored.

Notice how the term *cardiopulmonary resuscitation* is explained for readers. It's something you do "to circulate blood and provide oxygen until heart and lung function can be restored."

New words are often explained this way in textbooks too. The authors of textbooks don't expect you to know all the words they use. Nor do they expect you to stop and look them up. So they explain many of them as they go along.

Take the following passage from a biology book, for example. It introduces the word *metabolism*. This is a new word for most students. So the author defines it for readers in context. Watch for its meaning as you read the passage:

Malaria is a dramatic disease. In a typical attack, the victim first feels a severe chill. Gooseflesh forms, and his teeth chatter violently. Several hours later the sufferer feels very hot. He probably has a terrible headache and a feeling of nausea. Still later he begins to sweat. Clearly, the person's metabolism-that is, the way the parts of his body are working together-has been greatly upset by the disease.

Notice how the author defines the word *metabolism* for the reader. Metabolism means "the way the parts of the body are working together." As an example, the author describes how the disease upsets the normal process.

Using Synonyms and Explanations as Context Clues

Exercise C

Explanations and definitions that are provided by the author are an important source of information about new words and phrases. Practice using these context clues when you do Exercise C.

Read the news article carefully and answer the questions which follow.

Tricks of the Trade

Jungle cats leap through hoops of fire. Horses prance in a circle, nose to tail, then fall into place for a dance. Trained chimps perform alongside clowns and acrobats. To the audience, it's a wonder. To the trainer, it's the end result of a long education that began when the animals were young. The process is called *behavior modification*, because the trainer is *modifying*, or changing, the animal's behavior.

It starts with one small, easy lesson. A tiger cub, for instance, is taught to make a very short leap. A meat treat, lots of petting, and words of praise follow. These are known as *positive rewards*—good things that happen when an animal does what it is supposed to. The next time the tiger is encouraged to make a longer leap. Gradually the leaps become even longer and higher. Soon you hold out something for the tiger to jump through, like a hoop.

Of course, there are always problems along the way. The tiger may decide to jump around the hoop instead of through it. When this happens, the trainer gives the animal a few sharp taps with the side of a stick. This is an example of a *negative reward*—something unpleasant that follows a wrong move. The important thing is not to lose your temper. It only sets back the learning process. "I may lose my temper with my kids," says one top trainer, "but never with my animals."

As soon as the animal corrects its mistake, the praise and treats begin again. It can take up to two years. But one day it all comes together. And the wonder of it is—it looks so easy!

1. When you modify something, you (circle one)

   a. mistreat it   c. change it

   b. ignore it   d. introduce it

2. The meaning of the term "positive reward" is provided by the author in the context of the article. Find the meaning and write it below. _____

   _____

   _____

3. The term "negative reward" is also defined in context. Write its meaning on the lines below.

   _____

   _____

   _____

Using Synonyms and Explanations as Context Clues

Practice Using Your Newspaper

1. Choose an article in your newspaper that deals with either medicine or science and do the following:

   a. Find a word relating to medicine or science that is explained in the context of the article. Write down the word and the definition you find. _____

   _____

   _____

   b. In the same article, find a word whose meaning you are not sure of, and that is not explained in context. Look up its meaning in a dictionary. Then write a sentence you could insert in the article that defines this word for readers.

   Word: _____

   Dictionary definition: _____

   Sentence explaining this word that you could insert in the article:

   _____

   _____

   _____

2. Locate a gardening article or an article about the weather, and do the following:

   a. Circle as many adjectives as you can find. (Adjectives describe things–bright, colorful, icy, foggy, are examples of adjectives.)

   b. For each adjective, think of another word which has a similar or related meaning (a synonym).

   c. Re-write the sentence containing the adjective, this time adding the second adjective you chose.

   Example: "Keep *harmful* insects away from your vegetable garden by planting *pungent* marigolds at the ends of each row." "Keep harmful, *damaging* insects away from your vegetable garden by planting pungent, *strong-smelling* marigolds at the ends of the rows."

Now Try Your Newspower

Start one or more lists of words that belong to special vocabularies. These, you will recall, are words that apply mainly to one subject–sports, medicine, science, government, and so on. Keep each list on a separate sheet in your notebook. Whenever you read the newspaper, watch for words to add to your list. Enter them on the proper sheet, followed by a short definition. For example, your sports sheet might start something like this:

Sports Words

playoff–when two winning teams play against each other.

turnover–when possession of the ball changes from one team to the other.

Understanding Familiar Words Used in New Ways

Sometimes you meet a word you know perfectly well, yet it seems to have a different meaning.

Take the word *saddle*. Everyone knows that a saddle is a leather seat strapped onto a horse's back. But that is not its meaning in this sentence:

"Don't *saddle* me with your problems."

No one's talking about horseback riding here. The word's more common meaning, however, gives you a clue to its meaning in this context. A saddle is put on a horse's back. So when someone says, "Don't saddle me with your problems," they mean "Don't put your problems on my back."

Most words have more than one meaning, and that means they can be used in more that one way. Sometimes a word's different meanings may be totally unrelated. But frequently, like the word "saddle," the different meanings are related. Thus, if you know one meaning, and you study the way it is used in context, you can usually guess at its new meaning.

Here's another example of a familiar word used in a new way. Try to decide what the word *magnet* means in the following context:

Inner-city School to Open

SPRINGFIELD—The Board of Education today announced construction of a new magnet school to be located in downtown Springfield. The new school will offer an olympic-size pool, a revolving stage, a recording studio, and a fully equipped computer lab. A student-teacher ratio of ten to one means no class will have more than ten students. "We expect this school to attract students from all parts of the city," says spokesman Walt Jefferson. "Students and their parents will be banging on the doors to get in!" The school is expected to be completed in time for a September opening.

A magnet, as you probably know, exerts a force that attracts iron. This school, it seems, attracts students. It does this by offering special equipment and small classes. School officials hope to "draw in" students from all parts of the city. So they call it a *magnet school*.

It helps to form a picture in your mind and see where this leads you. Try it with the word "snowball." It's a familiar word, but look how it's used here:

The congressman's problems are expected to *snowball* as the scandal unfolds.

Picture in your mind a snowball being rolled downhill. As it moves it picks up more snow, getting bigger and bigger. This is a clue to the word's other meaning. Problems that "snowball" are problems that keep growing bigger.

It works the same way with the word "blanket." "This car comes with a *blanket* guarantee!" says the salesman. A blanket guarantee? One that covers everything–like a blanket.

Sometimes it takes a leap of the imagination to understand these words you "know but don't know." But if you can relate their familiar, everyday meaning to their new use, then you have mastered another important context clue.

Understanding Familiar Words Used in New Ways

Exercise D

Read the news article and answer the questions that follow.

New Hope for the Middle East

Leaders from the Middle East met to *bridge* their differences at a mini *summit* meeting this week held at Foster Hall at Masillion University. The meeting was sponsored by the International League for Worldwide Understanding. "At the very least," said one spokesman, "we think we have laid a *foundation* for future talks. Our hope, of course, is that this meeting will prove to be a *springboard* for peace." White House officials say they favor such as a meeting and look forward to similar meetings in the future.

Because of threats made by several terrorist organizations, security at the university was extremely tight during the meetings. Thanks to the vigilance of security officers, there were no incidents and the meeting went off without a hitch.

1. The way it is used here, the word "bridge" means

   [ ] a. to build a road across a body of water.

   [ ] b. to find a way over or around.

   [ ] c. to pretend a problem that isn't there.

   [ ] d. to come before a judge.

2. The word *summit* means "the top." What does this tell you about a summit meeting?

   _____

   _____

   _____

3. A *foundation* is the solid structure on which a house rests. What does a house foundation have in common with a "*foundation* for further talks"?

   [ ] a. They're both hidden from view.

   [ ] b. They will both crumble.

   [ ] c. They're both a base to build upon.

   [ ] d. They're both made of concrete.

4. A diving *springboard* helps divers to leap higher and perform a better dive. How might you define a *springboard* for peace?

   _____

   _____

Understanding Familiar Words Used in New Ways

Practice Using Your Newspaper

Turn to the entertainment pages of your newspaper (where they write about TV shows and movies). Read at least two articles and do the following:

1. Make a list of words you come across that you associate with this area–words like film, chorus, star, and so on.

2. Write a sentence using this word with its familiar meaning. (You can also use the sentence in which you found the word.)

3. Write another sentence using this same word, but in a different context with a different meaning.

The first one is done for you as an example.

Word: __film__   Familiar use: __Movie director George Lucas is making a new film__

__about outer space.__

Different use: __There is a film of dirt on this window.__

Word: _____ Familiar use: _____

_____

Different use: _____

Word: _____ Familiar use: _____

_____

Different use: _____

Word: _____ Familiar use: _____

_____

Different use: _____

Word: _____ Familiar use: _____

_____

Different use: _____

Word: _____ Familiar use: _____

_____

Different use: _____

Understanding Familiar Words Used in New Ways

Now Try Your Newspower

Start a collection of words you come across in your newspaper reading that seem to be used in new, imaginative ways. Write down the sentence or phrase which contains the word. Find out what it means when it is used this way, and write this new definition on the next line. Your list might start out like this:

Common Words Used in New Ways

to *trigger* a recession—You pull the trigger to start a gun. So to trigger a recession means to start a recession.

a *steering* committee—To steer something means to point it in a certain direction. So a steering committee decides what goals or course of action an organization should take.

jackrabbit starts and stops—A jackrabbit starts and stops very suddenly. So jackrabbit starts and stops are sudden starts and stops.

a *bull* market—a *bear* market—See if you can learn the imaginative meanings of these two stock market terms.

Add Your Own (Continue with words you find yourself.)

Phrase: _____

Meaning in this context: _____

_____

New definition: _____

_____

Phrase: _____

Meaning in this context: _____

_____

New definition: _____

_____

_____

Phrase: _____

Meaning in this context: _____

_____

New definition: _____

_____

For Words You Still Don't Understand...

Sometimes there are just no context clues and you'll find yourself stumped by a new word. When this happens, you have a decision to make: Should you stop and look it up, or go on reading?

Surprisingly, reaching for the dictionary is not always the best choice. It interrupts your train of thought, for one thing. And for another, it breaks into the mood of a good story and spoils your pleasure. So you should stop to look up a word only when it's important. How can you tell when a word is important enough to pause over? Two questions can help you decide. Ask yourself these two questions, which can help you decide:

---

1. Can you explain what the main idea of the reading is without knowing the meaning of this word?

2. Does the sentence or passage still make sense if you leave out this word?

If you can answer yes to both questions, then it is probably okay to look it up later. (Make a note of it, meanwhile, so you don't forget.) But if you can't get the gist of what the author is saying without knowing what a certain word means, then you should reach for your dictionary.

For example, if you are reading an article about generic drugs, you need to know that *generic* means a general name as opposed to a brand name. If this is not explained in context, then you should stop and look it up.

Some words are essential to the meaning of a sentence. If a sentence makes no sense without this word, then obviously you want to know its meaning. The word *assiduous* in the next sentence is a good example of this:

The receptionist was assiduous about performing her duties.

Was she a good receptionist or a poor one? Unless you know that assiduous means diligent and hard working, this sentence will have no meaning for you.

Other words are not so vital to the meaning of the sentence. For example:

The vandals were suspended from school for their wanton **act of destruction.**

The word *wanton* (it means without reason) adds meaning to this sentence. But the sentence still makes sense without it: "The vandals were suspended from school for their act of destruction." So this is a word you could decide to look up later.

Practice making these kinds of decisions as you read the article on page 47.

For Words You Still Don't Understand...

Exercise E

The following article contains a number of words (in bold type) you may not know. Some are explained in context. Others are not. Complete the exercise at the bottom of the page by circling the correct choices.

Teens Take Fitness Tests

America's teens, by and large, are an **enervated** bunch. At least, that's the verdict of the President's Council of Physical Fitness and Sports. Almost half of those tested for **aerobic** endurance failed to meet minimum standards for their age group.

Experts blame schools for ending **mandatory** physical education. Gym classes have been among the **frivolous** courses cut so money could be diverted to **fundamental** courses such as science, math, reading and writing.

"Some of these kids don't even know what it means to feel fit," says one coach who participated in the study. "Fitness is more than the absence of blubber. Fit means having a high energy level, enthusiasm and **zest** for living. You don't feel tired after school."

Or in school either, say some educators. "You need just as much stamina to tackle your studies as to tackle your opponent on the playing field." Indeed, fitness is part of a new holistic approach to education.

1. It is important to know what the word enervated means because (choose 2)
   a. this first sentence expresses the main idea of the article.
   b. it is a multisyllabic word.
   c. the sentence makes little sense without it.
   d. adjectives should always be looked up.

2. The subject of this article is a clue that a test for aerobic endurance is probably a test of
   a. intelligence.
   b. physical attractiveness.
   c. potential for success.
   d. physical fitness.

3. What can you conclude about the word mandatory in the sentence, "Experts blame schools for ending mandatory physical education"?
   a. It probably means the same thing as physical.
   b. Check it later. You can get most of the idea without it.
   c. You should stop and look it up if you don't already know what it means.
   d. It has a threatening tone, so look it up at once.

4. From the context in which they are used, you could conclude that the words frivolous and fundamental mean
   a. about the same thing.
   b. about the opposite of each other.

5. Reread the third paragraph of the article, starting "Some of these kids..." Find a word which explains the word "zest." Write it on the line provided _____.

For Words You Still Don't Understand...

Practice Using Your Newspaper

Challenge your reading ability by reading a rather long article in your newspaper on a topic you don't understand too well. It may be about politics, science, the environment, or international affairs. Concentrate and try to become interested in the subject. Asking yourself questions about the subject as you read is one way to arouse your curiosity and interest. Or, read the article together with someone else and discuss it. Avoid reading easy articles about crime, sports, star gossip, or human interest. Do the following:

- Copy the headline.
- Tell in one short sentence what the article is about.
- As you read, circle words whose meanings you are not sure of.
- Make a list of these words, allowing two lines between words.
- First, guess at the meaning of each word from the way it is used in context. Write this meaning after the word.
- Look up each word in your dictionary and write the exact meaning on the next line. If there is more than one meaning in the dictionary be sure to choose the one meaning that works with the context of the article.
- If you can't guess the meaning of a word, and the reading doesn't make sense when you skip over the word, stop and check the word in your dictionary before going on.

Headline _____

What the article is about _____

Word list (with the meaning you guess at, and the dictionary definition): _____

_____

_____

_____

_____

Now Try Your Newspower

1. Select a subject from one of these:
   politics, international affairs, science, entertainment, the environment, business

2. For one week, read everything you can find in your newspaper about your subject.

3. Keep a list of words that relate to your subject. Guess their meanings from the way they are used in context, and check their exact meanings in your dictionary. Examples:
   Politics: filibuster, amendment, compromise, conservative...
   International affairs: Salt II, solidarity, détente, negotiations...
   Business: price index, mean, balance of payments...

4. Write a short essay (about 100 words) that tells about something interesting you found in your reading. Use as many as you can of the new words you learned in your reading.

Chapter 3: Making Inferences

Introduction

Making inferences is something that goes on inside your head, so like the word "thinking" it's rather hard to define. What happens when you think? No one really knows. It is much the same with making inferences. No one really knows how it is done, except that it's a thinking process–one you use every day.

An inference is a thought or an idea that you create from facts, or from other thoughts and ideas. You see, hear, or read certain facts, details, and ideas. You organize these in your mind and come to a conclusion. Or you create a new idea. You make an inference. Here is an example:

Several classmates in your homeroom are absent from school one morning. All of them live on South Mountain and come to school by bus. It is snowing. You *infer* from these facts that the bus is delayed or has been canceled due to the snow.

When you put the facts together to see where they lead you, you are making an inference.

1. Classmates are absent from school.

2. All of them ride the South Mountain bus.

3. It is snowing.

Now you go *beyond* these facts—one step further—to create a new idea. You infer the bus was delayed or canceled because of snow. This is not a fact that is set out for you. It is an idea you formed yourself based on facts. In other words, you *inferred* it.

Making inferences is a skill you use all the time, and you use all sorts of evidence to make inferences:

> **Facial expressions**. Your friend tries out for the lead in the school play. The results are posted and you see her frown as she reads the notice. You *infer* that she didn't get the part.

> **Tone of voice**. The telephone rings in another room and your mother answers it. You can't make out words, but you hear voice sounds that are tense and strained, even tearful. You *infer* that your mother has heard bad news.

> **Speech and behavior**. The new student speaks slowly and with a Swedish accent. He acts a bit shy and nervous. This, you *infer*, must be the exchange student from Sweden.

An inference is more than a guess or an assumption. It is more than a feeling or opinion. Inferences must be based on *evidence*. You might guess or assume that a certain shampoo is better than another because it costs more. But if you read the labels and compare the ingredients, you might infer from the evidence that there is very little difference.

Inferences are important in all kinds of reading. The words on the page may be only half the story. The other half of the story—often the most important half—comes from the inferences you make. Some people call this "reading between the lines" because inferences are not printed on the page. Inferences are read into a story when you put facts and details together, think about them, and see where they lead you.

Making inferences helps you to get the most out of an author's message. The following lessons show you how to make inferences from whatever you read.

Everything you read contains facts and details that provide information. But that's not all. The facts and details, even the words an author chooses, provide evidence that can be the basis for making inferences. "There's more to this than meets the eye" is a comment that might be made about almost any piece of writing.

Watch how it works in this news story about food tampering.

Metal Found in Candy Bar

Police are checking a complaint by Sarah Derevault, 16, of Birne City, that she found a jagged piece of metal when she bit into a candy bar she had just purchased. It was the latest in a long series of reports of food tampering.

From facts in just these two sentences you can make an important inference. If this is "the latest in a long series of reports of food tampering," you can infer that this has become a real problem. This idea isn't stated in so many words, but you can dig it out by thinking about what has been said. You can "read between the lines." The story continues.

Some foreign matter in food products are probably the result of minor plant accidents. "From time to time a piece of wire from a brush, or metal shavings from machinery get into food," investigators say. But items such as needles and large pieces of jagged metal are rarely accidents. These things must be deliberately introduced into food.

There are at least two more inferences to be made as you think about what you have read. Since the investigators talk about plant accidents "from time to time," you can infer that foreign matter turns up in food more or less regularly. It just can't be helped in a large manufacturing process. You may make a mental note to yourself to be just a bit cautious about anything you eat.

Then you notice the article began by talking about a jagged piece of metal, and later needles are mentioned. So you can infer that at some time needles have been found in food as well as jagged metal.

As you think about it some more, you realize that it would be very difficult to put a piece of jagged metal in a candy bar after it has been wrapped and packaged. So, you may infer, the metal probably was introduced before it was wrapped. A needle, on the other hand, can be inserted through a package after it has been wrapped.

These are all inferences inspired by the facts. They are ideas that were not stated. You had to dig them out yourself in the same way that a detective goes after clues.

Reading Between the Lines

Exercise A

This exercise gives you practice in making inferences from information you find in your reading.

Read the entire news article. Then answer the questions that follow. Notice that each part of the article is numbered—part 1, part 2, etc. At the beginning of each question you are told which part of the article the question refers to. Reread this part of the article carefully before you answer the question.

Double Trouble from Sports Injuries

Part 1

"Aw, it's just a sprain, coach," the young athlete says. "I'm okay." and with just a bit of a limp he runs back to finish the game. He might also be finishing his career as an athlete.

Part 2

A sprain is not something to be taken lightly. When a body joint is sprained—ankle, knee, elbow, or shoulder—it means considerable damage has been done. The joint has been twisted far beyond its limits so that the tough connecting tissues that hold the bones together are torn. In terms of giving life-long pain and trouble, sprains can be more serious than a broken bone. So when a sprain occurs, you must stop using the injured part at once and get help from a doctor.

In the heat of a game a player may think a twisted knee or ankle is hurt less than it is. By continuing to play, more damage is done. Many a young athlete who has done this finds out later he has a "trick knee" that plagues him for the rest of his life.

Part 3

Breaks near the ends of the long bones are very serious for young people under sixteen. These should be treated by a doctor who is a bone specialist and then watched for a number of years to see that no problems develop.

Bones in people who are still

Veterinarian treating a patient.   Photo by Stan Sherer

growing have "growth plates" near the ends. These allow the bones to grow as the rest of the body grows. When a growth plate is damaged, a bone will tend to grow faster or slower than it is supposed to.

Part 4

Young athletes are not protected from sports injuries as well as adults and professionals for a number of reasons. Equipment of school and sandlot teams is not as good as that of the professionals. Kids' teams don't have doctors or trainers. Some coaches push kids harder than they should be pushed. For these and other reasons, many doctors advise careful regulation of body contact sports played by people under college age.

Reading Between the Lines

Exercise A *(cont.)*

Part 1

Reread Part 1 of the news article. What can you infer from the sentence: "He might also be finishing his career as an athlete"?

( ) a. The game will soon be over.

( ) b. The player will soon graduate and so end his school athletic career.

( ) c. The injury might be very serious.

( ) d. The career of an athlete is never very long.

Part 2

Reread Part 2 of the news article. Use inference to decide which one of the following statements is most likely to be true.

( ) a. Most sprains can be cured by putting ice on the injury.

( ) b. Sprains may give trouble years after they happen.

( ) c. You are a crybaby if you go to a doctor because of a little sprain.

( ) d. A "trick knee" is something caused by old age.

Part 3

Reread Part 3 of the news article. You are not told, so you have to infer what may happen if the bone in one leg grows faster than the bone in the other leg as the result of an injury. What can you infer?

( ) a. One leg may become shorter than the other resulting in a limp.

( ) b. You may become taller or shorter than you should be.

( ) c. It will result in an incurable disease.

( ) d. The other bones in the body will probably stop growing.

Part 4

Reread Part 4 of the news article. Which one of the following statements is a reasonable inference you can make as a result of what you read?

( ) a. Every sandlot team should have a doctor present at all games.

( ) b. People under college age should not play body contact sports.

( ) c. Little league and high school athletes shouldn't be pushed as hard as college and professional players.

( ) d. High school and little league teams should be regulated by having them get licenses from the state.

Reading Between the Lines

Practice Using Your Newspaper

Select two articles from your newspaper that you find interesting. For each article do the following:

1. Copy one important fact or idea that is clearly stated in the article.

2. In your own words, write a second idea that the writer doesn't come right out and tell you, but an idea or thought you can "dig out" using inference.

Example:

College to Admit Women

Lorenz University, one of only two all-male colleges in the country, decided Saturday they will admit women students for the first time this fall. Like many other schools, Lorenz is becoming concerned that there will be fewer high school graduates in the future to fill all the places available in more than 2000 colleges nationwide.

A fact that is stated: *Lorenz University will admit women for the first time.*

An idea you infer: *Lorenz is taking women to fill up classes that might not have enough students otherwise.*

Article 1:

A fact that is stated: _____

_____

_____

An idea you infer: _____

_____

_____

Article 2:

A fact that is stated: _____

_____

_____

An idea you infer: _____

_____

Reading Between the Lines

1. Select an article from your newspaper that you feel is important.
2. Write a one page essay. Title your essay like this:
   - Use the headline of the article as the main title of your essay.
   - Use the following words as your second title or subtitle: "What It Means To Me." Example:
   U.S.–Soviets To Improve Relations—What It Means To Me
3. After you have finished your essay, reread it carefully. In the margin of your paper, mark the facts and ideas you found stated clearly in the article. Label these *f* and *i* (facts and ideas). Then find ideas that are your own inferences, based on facts and ideas in the article. Label these ***infer.***
4. It will be interesting to compare your inferences with others who have written about the same newspaper article.

—What It Means To Me

(Title)

_____

_____

_____

_____

_____

_____

_____

_____

_____

_____

_____

_____

_____

_____

_____

_____

How To Make an Inference

As we have already pointed out, making inferences is a part of the thinking you do in everyday life. You can infer that someone is angry with you by the way they speak and act toward you. The tone of voice and the person's actions are the evidence from which you make your inference. You may infer someone is trying to fool you when what they say does not match with the facts of what they do. From certain signs (evidence) in nature you can infer that winter is almost over and spring is just around the coner.

These are things you think about without even being aware you are doing something special. You do the same thing as you read. But many times in reading it pays to be more aware of making inferences. When you read for a history test, when you want to decide who to vote for, or what you believe about an important issue, you need to think more carefully about what you read. You want to make your inferences in a more thoughtful and organized way.

What follows is a formula or "recipe" for making inferences when you read. Once you get the hang of it, though, you won't need a formula. Inferences will come as naturally as eating and sleeping.

Steps in Making an Inference

1. Notice facts and ideas with an eagle eye. Decide which facts and ideas are most important.

2. Decide where the facts and ideas are leading.

3. Make your inferences. To do this, go a step beyond the facts and ideas in the reading to create ideas of your own. Remember–in order to be inferences, these new ideas must be based on evidence you find in the article. Feelings, guesses, and opinions don't count as inferences.

Read the following news article carefully. See what inferences you can make from it. Following the article there is a step-by-step analysis leading to some of the inferences you can make.

Flying Trains Tested

TOKYO—The Japanese think trains should fly like airplanes, so their space-age engineers have built a train that cruises at more that 300 miles per hour.

The ML train (the initials stand for magnetically levitated) sailed through the air about four inches above the roadbed. The train starts out on its wheels, but when it reaches a speed of 100 mph the wheels retract like those of an airplane, and the train skims through the air. The ride is smoother than an airplane, however, because there are no sudden ups and downs.

The fate of the ML's now passes from the engineers to the taxpayers. The engineers have proved that it works. But the construction costs are enormous.

Important facts and ideas

*   Japanese engineers have built a new high-speed train.

*   Construction costs are enormous.

How To Make an Inference

Steps In Making an Inference (cont.)

Where are the facts leading?

- Will we soon be traveling on such trains?
- Would such trains be a benefit to our country?

Making inferences—thoughts of your own

- Because ML's are fast and give a smooth ride, they could attract more people to use trains.
- Because costs are enormous, chances are we won't see ML's operating here soon.

Examples of ideas that are not inferences

- It will be a lot safer to float on a cushion of air than to ride on rails.
- We probably won't get ML's because the auto companies will object.

These are guesses, feelings, or opinions. Nothing in the article can lead you to these ideas.

Following are two items from a newspaper. The first is a news article about a man who claims to have been attacked by wolves. The second is an angry letter from a reader about the news article. What can you infer about this situation after reading both items? Follow the same steps in making an inference as you did in the example above.

Man Attacked by Wolves

WEIRS POINT, N.J.—John Loftstrum, a local hunter and sportsman, reported to local police that he and his dog were attacked by wolves as they walked near the border of the state forest adjoining his home. "These weren't coyotes or coy-dogs or anything like that," he said. "These were full-size timber wolves."

Loftstrum reported that his dog was running ahead of him when two wolves appeared and attacked the dog. He said he beat the wolves off with a tree limb, but not before both he and his dog were badly bitten. A hunting party has been formed to track down the wolves.

Letters To The Editor

No Wolves in New Jersey

Your article about the man who was attacked by "wolves" should have included the fact that there haven't been any wolves in New Jersey for more than a hundred years. The man was probably attacked by wild dogs. We have lots of those, thanks to thoughtless owners who turn unwanted pets out to fend for themselves.

Phony stories about wolves have been around as long as Little Red Riding Hood. Most of the time wolves keep away from people if they can. If the town would enforce its leash laws we wouldn't need any "wolf" hunts.

Mrs. Sharon Wills

How To Make an Inference

Read the following feature story. Then use the steps for making inferences to complete the exercise below.

The Wonderful Baobab

by Linten Rockwell

What tree can be lived in, and used for clothing, food, dinnerware, seasonings, and medicine? There's only one. The wonderful baobab (pronounced Bay-oh-Bab).

The first time you see a baobab, you may get the feeling you are looking at something slightly unreal. It has a huge trunk, second in size only to the great sequoias of California. It's not very tall for its great width, however, so it has a rather squat appearance. The roots grow high into the trunk of the tree and spread out in a tangle along the ground like long tentacles. Higher up it seems to have a shaggy mane that's badly in need of a haircut.

The tree is found in Africa and India where, years gone by, people lived in baobabs they had hollowed out by hand. Surprisingly, the baobab often continued to live itself, producing fruits for the occupants of its insides. The bark is very fibrous, so it can be made into thread and then into cloth. Seasoning for food and medicines can be made from the tree's leaves.

If you need food to use with the seasoning, the tree is happy to oblige. It has a fruit that is gourd-shaped and quite tasty. The gourds themselves can be used, once they have been emptied and dried, for a variety of household items from dishes to drinking vessels. Someone once said that when you live in a baobab, the only thing you don't get from the tree is a rent bill.

Notice important facts

1. List as many facts as you can find in the article that describes a baobab and what can be done with it. _____

_____

_____

Where the facts are leading

2. The facts lead to:

   a. the idea that the baobab is an endangered species.

   b. an argument that baobabs can solve world hunger problems.

   c. the idea that the baobab is a tree with many uses.

Making inferences

3. a. Sequoias are mentioned in the article. You are not told what a sequoia is, but you can *infer* it is a tree. You can also *infer* which tree is taller–a sequoia or a baobab.

   _____

   _____

   b. Copy the sentences that enable you to infer which tree is taller. Use the back of this paper.

4. Using facts, infer where a baobab would be most useful, in an industrial or a developing country? _____

How To Make an Inference

Practice Using Your Newspaper

1. Select two fairly long articles from your newspaper that you find interesting.

2. Use the steps for making inferences to develop some good ideas of your own about the article.

These ideas should be inferences, not feelings, guesses, or opinions.

Article I

Some important facts _____

_____

_____

Where are the facts leading? _____

_____

_____

Your inferences _____

_____

_____

Article 2

Some important facts _____

_____

_____

Where are the facts leading? _____

_____

_____

Your inferences _____

_____

Now Try Your Newspower

1. Read any article from your newspaper that you find interesting. For this exercise, two or more people should read the same article.

2. Each person should write down an inference that can be made from reading the article.

3. Each person examines the inferences others have written. Discuss the inferences to decide if they are true inferences; that is, be sure there is evidence in the article that leads to the inference that has been made.

Tone is a term people often use when talking about music: "The fife piped in with its high, shrill tones." Or, "the low rumble of muffled drums gave a somber tone to the funeral march."

We also talk about tone of voice–not a singing voice, necessarily, but the way people sound when they speak. "Don't use that tone of voice with me!" is a remark most of us have heard after using a rude or sassy tone to someone.

There are as many tones to a speaking voice as there are tones of music. A person's voice can sound sweet, cheerful, hateful, disappointed, angry, and so on. These tones of voice can be expressed in writing as well as spoken. And when you sense a certain tone in your reading, you can often make an inference based upon it.

Remember that one of the steps in making an inference asks you to decide where the facts and ideas are leading. Writers often use tone to lead you where they want you to go with your thinking. They try to influence your inferences, in other words. This can be helpful, but you have to be careful. Some writers use tone to lead your inferences to conclusions that are rather far from the truth.

In order to recognize tone in what you read, try to identify the author's feeling toward the subject. Is the writer for a proposal or against it? Is he or she writing a frank discussion or is he or she speaking with hatred? Is the writer amused or upset?

Read the following letter to the editor. How does the writer feel? And where is he trying to lead you with his tone?

Reader Disgusted by Show

I enjoy state fairs and carnivals, and I'm still young enough to enjoy the midway rides and shows. But I must say there was one show this year that can only be called disgusting. It was a freak show. For a dollar you can go into the tent to look at a group of people. It made me sick.

It's bad enough that these unfortunate people were born with severe physical handicaps. But to put them on display like strange animals is horrible and inhuman. It ruined my whole day at the fair.

I think shows that take advantage of disabled people should not be allowed to play in our city.

David Durmer

The evidence of this author's tone allows you to infer that he is angry, disgusted, and disapproving. The words *sick, disgusting, horrible*, and *inhuman* help create the tone.

What is more, the author is leading you with his tone to try to make you feel the same way he does. If you tend to agree with the writer, you might infer that whoever runs the side show is an evil, uncaring person. But what do you infer from the tone of a letter the side show owner wrote in reply to David Durmer?

Making inferences from Tone

Side Show People Care

I'm sorry Mr. Durmer was upset with our show. But I want him and your readers to know that we do not mistreat our people. Effie our fat lady weighs 650 pounds. She is alone in the world and her only income is from what the show brings her.

Sam, whose deformity is a pin-shaped or pointed head, is also mentally handicapped as a result of this defect. But he gets a salary, he has good food and a clean place to live, and he is among people who love him and care for him.

The stories of other people in our show are much the same. As far as I'm concerned they are leading happy, useful lives, and people who think themselves good-hearted should not try to take this away from them.

Simon Medlow

The letter has a calm, reasoning tone. This writer is trying to lead readers to make entirely different inferences about side shows. From the information given, and the reasonable tone, the writer wants you to infer that all is right with his people. The tone as well as the facts he presents lead you to your inferences.

Newspaper columnists also use tone to lead a reader's thinking.

On the Trail Again

Well, Phineas Bloomer is on the campaign trail again and tossing out promises like bridal bouquets. He'd promise to paint the White House pink if he thought it would win him an extra vote.

His latest promise is that he will do something "soon" about workers' safety. (This said to a gathering of construction workers.) He neglected to mention that just such a bill has been bottled up in his committee for nine months and he has done nothing about it.

This writer has provided facts to help you make your inferences. But he is also helping you along with a sarcastic tone. You may infer the writer doesn't think much of Phineas Bloomer from the tone. Then he throws in a fact to support his feeling: Mr. Bloomer says one thing to the workers, but he does another thing in his committee.

Making Inferences from Tone

Now compare the next two articles. They are about the same thing, but one has a neutral tone, while the other is slanted to affect your feelings.

Village Bombed

COSTA COBRENO—Rebel forces led by Paolo Navarra bombed a remote village yesterday, killing ten people and injuring 30.

In this short item, all you have are some facts about a bombing. The tone is neutral. Any inferences you make will have to be based on these facts alone. Most news articles are written this way. But read it written a different way:

Village Bombed

Costa Cobreno—*Terrorists* belonging to the *outlawed* forces of Paolo Navarra bombed a *defenseless* village today, *murdering* ten innocent victims and maiming at least 30 *others*.

Now the writer is telling you he wants you to infer the bombing was an outrage, a crime against humanity. The author has used the words *terrorists, outlawed, defenseless, murdering,* and *others* to make you feel this way.

From the first article you infer that another tragedy has occurred in the world. Since it happened in a village, it is likely that innocent people were involved.

You can make the same inferences from the second article. But now you can also infer that whoever wrote the article doesn't like Paolo Navarra and his rebels.

This is the difference between *objective* writing, where just facts are reported, and *subjective* writing, where the writer allows his feelings to show through the writing in his tone.

Making Inferences from Tone

Exercise C

Read the following letter to the editor. Pay attention to the tone of each letter. Notice words and expressions that create the tone. Then complete the exercise that follows.

Save the Trees

Maple Street got its name from the beautiful trees that have grown there for more than 100 years. Now the city fathers in their great wisdom have decided the trees must go. They are in the way of "progress."

"Progress" comes in the form of widening Maple Street to provide better access to and from the new Oxford Shopping Mall. When the street is widened the stately old maples lining the street will be sacrificed. This will make Maple Street part of the asphalt desert the mall already is. This is a sneak attack by the city and the mall developers. No mention of destroying Maple Street was made in the original plans for the mall that was approved by the city council. Suddenly the trees must go. As far as I'm concerned the new Oxford Mall can go!

Jane Lazzard

1. Jane Lazzard says, "the city fathers in their great wisdom. . ." You can infer from her tone that she thinks the city fathers are:

   ( ) just and wise.

   ( ) progressive thinkers.

   ( ) not wise in this case.

   ( ) overly cautious.

2. What words and expressions used by Jane Lazzard lead you to infer that Maple Street will be an awful place without trees? Write down at least one expression she uses to do this.

   _____

   _____

   _____

3. Choose two or three facts or ideas from the letter that you can use objectively (without tone or coloring) to make inferences about the situation on Maple Street. Example: When the street is widened the trees must go.

   _____

   _____

   _____

Making Inferences from Tone

Practice Using Your Newspaper

Find an article in your newspaper that is an example of objective writing. Objective writing presents facts that are not colored by the writer's tone (his or her feelings). News articles are usually written objectively. Mark the article you select—OBJECTIVE.

Find an article that is an example of **subjective** writing. This kind of writing is colored by the writer's feelings. You can find this kind of writing in an editorial or in an opinion column that deals with politics, entertainment, food, sports, or some other topic. Mark this article-SUBJECTIVE.

Do the following:

1. Make an inference of your own based on information in the OBJECTIVE article. _____

    _____

2. Tell what the writer wants you to infer from the way he or she presents the information in the SUBJECTIVE article.
   (Examples: The writer wants you to infer someone acted improperly. The writer wants you to infer something is good or bad.) _____

    _____

3. Copy at least one sentence from the SUBJECTIVE article that shows how the writer uses tone to lead or direct the inferences you make.
   (Example: In an outstandingly poor performance, Rod Philstrom pitched the worst game of his career.) _____

    _____

    _____

    _____

    _____

    _____

    _____

    _____

Now Try Your Newspower

1. Reread the OBJECTIVE newspaper article you selected for Practice Using Your Newspaper (above.)
2. Rewrite this article so that it provides the same information, but color it with feelings. In other words, provide a tone for the article that makes it *subjective*.
   Example
   Objective: The Tower Hills nuclear power plant will be operating at full capacity tomorrow following a three-day shutdown. A crack that was discovered in a metal pump has now been repaired, officials of the plant say.
   Rewritten subjectively: The Tower Hills nuclear plant will once again threaten the area when it begins to operate at full capacity tomorrow. A dangerous crack was discovered in a metal pump. If plant officials can be believed, the pump has been repaired.
3. Optional Exercise. Try to rewrite the article a second way to lead a reader in another *direction*.

Inferences can only be made from information you have on hand. If facts are wrong or ideas are colored to influence your thinking, the inferences you make will be flawed or slanted. It's not your fault as a reader. You have done nothing wrong. The inferences you make are probably correct, given the facts you have to work with. But you may have been misled by the writer, accidentally or purposely.

This is often easy to see in political speeches and some advertisements. Facts can be colored by tone, as you saw in the last lesson. Facts and ideas may be exaggerated. Important facts you need to make an inference may be left out. And there's always the danger that you are being deliberately deceived with false information.

The following advertisement wants you to infer that a very superior pair of jogging shoes is being offered at a very low price. But if you examine the information carefully, you have good reason to question this inference. As you read the ad, consider both facts that are included, and facts that have been *left out*.

SAVE! SAVE! SAVE!
Famous A-Deed-a Joggers—now ½ off—
$7.95

These nylon and leather-look joggers have been tested by an independent laboratory with superior results.

Here are some *incorrect* inferences you can make from this ad:

- You may infer that the store is offering a well-known shoe as they say. Adidas is a famous brand. But this is A-Deed-a, a play on the famous name.

- ½ off, you may infer, is a bargain. This is a comparison often used in advertising that is not a comparison at all. You are not told what this price is half of. It's roughly half of $16, but there's no evidence these shoes were ever that price.

Examining Inferences

- "Leather-look" is not the same as leather. The ad writer would like you to infer that it is, however.

- You are asked to infer that the shoes were submitted to rigorous testing and found to be good, long-lasting shoes. You are told the results were superior–but you are not told superior to what (to sandals or slippers, perhaps?). You are not even told what the laboratory was testing for.

The message is not false advertising. What happens is that you are given just enough information to help you to mislead yourself into making incorrect inferences.

Now see how you can make two opposite inferences about the famous Woodstock music festival of 1969 from the following articles.

Woodstock Remembered

The great Woodstock rock festival of 1969 was an historic event best remembered for its outpouring of feelings of peace and love. It is also remembered for the appearance in one place of some of the greatest rock musicians of that most famous era of rock music: Jimi Hendrix; The Who; Janis Joplin; Jefferson Airplane; Crosby, Stills, Nash, and Young, and many others.

It was expected that the concert would turn into a disastrous riot. Almost a half million people showed up in a place where only 50,000 were expected. But the spirit of cooperation was something that is not likely to be seen again in this country.

Remembering Woodstock

The Woodstock rock festival of 1969 was not held at Woodstock at all, but in the town of Bethel, N.Y., which had the affair thrust on it after Woodstock refused to issue a permit.

Crowds overflowed the 640-acre site rented for the occasion. Food and water was scarce and toilet facilities were minimal. Chaos was everywhere and young people present didn't seem to care. In the middle of the madness it rained, turning the place into a sea of mud.

Residents of Bethel would like to forget the nightmare of those three days, calling it the worst party and the greatest pile of filth since the fall of the Roman Empire.

Each of the articles gives you a different set of facts to work with. Both sets of facts are essentially correct. But because the facts are different you must come away with different inferences. In the first case you infer that Woodstock was probably a wonderful experience for the young people attending. The second article leads you to infer it was a nightmarish time for the people of Bethel, N.Y., where the concert was held.

Both inferences are probably correct. And if you put the facts of both articles together, you can come up with another inference. Something like this: There were a lot of problems at the Woodstock festival, and it is remembered differently by different people, depending on how they were involved.

Examining Inferences

Exercise D

Following are common types of advertising. While the ads are entirely honest as far as truth in advertising laws are concerned, the advertisers lead you to make inferences that aren't always correct. Read each advertisement carefully. Decide what the advertiser **wants** you to infer. Then try to make a more accurate inference based on the information given you.

1. You receive a notice in the mail. The advertiser is running a contest to encourage you to fill out an order form for magazines. The notice begins this way:

    "Because your lucky number has been drawn by our judges, you may already be the winner of $50,000! Return the enclosed coupon with your lucky number and your order for any of 100 exciting magazines at tremendous savings, and you will become eligible for the grand jackpot sweepstakes."

    A. What does the advertiser want you to infer about winning $50,000? _____

    _____

    B. What is a correct inference about winning $50,000? _____

    _____

    _____

2. A TV announcer says: *"Slim-Down Diet Capsules are guaranteed to help you lose weight in ten days!"* Which one of the following is a correct inference based on the information given you?

    ( ) a. Because the diet capsules are guaranteed, you will surely lose weight in ten days if you take these capsules.

    ( ) b. The diet capsules may help you lose weight, but you will probably have to do other things besides.

3. A magazine ad says: *"Zitz-Cure has been hospital-tested for effectiveness in the treatment of acne."* What can you infer about the effectiveness of Zitz-Cure from the information given?

    ( ) a. If Zitz-Cure has been tested in hospitals it will cure acne. This fact is guaranteed by truth-in-advertising laws.

    ( ) b. You can't infer anything because you don't have enough information. The ad doesn't say what the results of the test were.

4. Writers use so-called **qualifying** words when they want to avoid telling you that something always works, or something is **always** true. Words like **sometimes** and **often** (not always), **may be** (not sure), **virtually** (almost), are some of these words.

    In the following advertising blurb, the writer wants you to infer that Medication M is a strong, effective medicine. But there are so many qualifying words that it is impossible to make a true inference about the product. Write down the words that qualify the message, that is, the words that help the writer avoid saying anything is really true.

    "Medication M is the strongest and most effective medicine for pain relief that you can buy. Medication M often brings fast, temporary relief for minor aches and pains."

    _____

    _____

Examining Inferences

Practice Using Your Newspaper

Read a review of a movie or a television show on the entertainment page of your newspaper.

You should be able to infer easily from the reviewer's remarks whether he or she liked the show, disliked it, or felt some other way about it. Do the following:

1. Tell what you can infer about the reviewer liking the show, disliking it, or feeling some other way about it.

2. Copy a sentence or two from the article that shows the information that enabled you to make this inference about the reviewer's feelings.

3. You should be able to infer from the article if you would like the show. Tell what your feelings are. You don't have to agree with the reviewer.

4. There is always something you would like to know about the show that the reviewer doesn't tell you. Write down at least one more piece of information you would like to have that might help you make a better inference about the show.

The name of the show_____

How does the reviewer feel about the show? _____

_____

Some information that helped you infer how the reviewer feels _____

_____

_____

What are your feelings about the show? _____

_____

_____

What other information would you have liked the reviewer to give you?_____

_____

_____

Now Try Your Newspower

In order to understand the meaning of a political cartoon you must make inferences. The cartoonist leads you to make the inferences he or she wants you to make by the way the cartoon is drawn and by what he or she says. Cartoonists always exaggerate to make the point clear to you.

Do the following:

1. Study a political cartoon in your newspaper.

2. Tell what ideas the cartoonist wants you to infer.

3. Tell how he or she leads you to infer these ideas. For example, is it the way the characters look? Is it what is said in the caption? Is it the strange situation in which the cartoonist places the characters?

4. Tell whether or not you think the inferences the cartoonist wants you to make are good ones. In other words, do you agree with the cartoonist?

5. Discuss the cartoon with others who have seen it. This may be a written or a class discussion exercise.

Chapter 4: Developing Critical Reading Skills

Introduction

Reading is more than simply passing your eyes over words, starting at the beginning of a chapter and stopping at the end. Reading is a thought process. So, in addition to plowing through words and sentences, you need to be thinking about what you are doing.

The first thing you want to think about is why you are reading the book or newspaper or magazine article that you have in front of you. You should have a reason for reading, in other words—a goal that you set for yourself. Learning facts and ideas, learning how to do something, reading to form an opinion, analyzing a character in a story, or simply reading to entertain yourself, are all worthwhile goals.

With a goal in mind, you have a better sense of what you are doing. You remember more of what you read. And having reached your goal, you are satisfied that you have accomplished what you set out to do.

Learning is always a goal of reading. This is true whether you read a schoolbook, a novel, or the comics in your newspaper. Many comic strips today have important ideas and opinions about the world we live in. Others make fun of habits and attitudes that are undesirable. You may laugh at "Hagar the Horrible," for example. But you also learn from this comic strip—if you think about it—that to be like Hagar is to be a ridiculous person.

The more you think about what you read, the more you learn. The lessons in this chapter will show you how to think about your reading in ways that will help you learn more, remember more, and accomplish the goals you set for yourself.

When you sit down to read something, you should have a purpose or goal in mind. If, when you finish your reading, you have accomplished your purpose, then you have met your reading goal. Here are some of the goals people set for themselves as they read:

- To gather ideas and information about a subject
- To learn how to do something
- To prepare for a test
- To form an opinion
- To relax and amuse yourself
- To stimulate your imagination and expand your mind

Having a goal helps you focus on your reading. If you are assembling a new bicycle from a set of instructions, your goal would be to fit the pieces together so the bike works well and safely. You would focus your attention, then, on the step-by-step procedure. You can have more than one goal as you read. But it is easier to begin with a single major goal and then relate other goals to it. For example, in assembling your bike, your major goal is to get it together and working. But you may also want to understand what each piece is for and how it functions. In this case, you may pause to puzzle over a more complicated part. Then you will fit it into your major goal of assembling the bike.

Setting Goals

Following is the beginning of an article about a potential disaster. Make a list of some of the goals you might set for yourself as you read.

Dam at Breaking Point

HUNTINGTON—Sixty-five residents of Huntington were evacuated yesterday when the Army Corps of Engineers determined that the near-by Ellmore Dam was in danger of bursting. "We're not taking any chances," says Mayor Sheila Armstrong, "which is why we're moving those people who are in the most danger. If the rain lets up in the next few days, we'll have a chance to lower the level of the reservoir behind the dam and start repairs."

If you live in Huntington, your goal would be to gather facts about the endangered dam and relate these facts to your own situation. Are you in danger? Do you know anyone else who is in danger? If you live elsewhere, you might be reading this article as a matter of human interest. If this were the case, you would focus on the dangers and hardships faced by the people of Huntington. If you are studying water control in your own community, your goal might be to compare what is happening in your town with what is going on in Huntington. If your goal is to learn about dams, you would concentrate on the report of the engineers. When you have a goal, you can focus on the information that is most important to you.

Keeping Your Goal in View

It's easy to keep track of your reading goals if you are reading only one article. But suppose you are reading a science textbook and you are learning about simple machines. This unit may cover 40 pages or more, and various reading assignments may be given over two weeks.

Your major goal will be to learn as much as you can about simple machines. Each reading assignment will have its own goal, however: learning about inclined planes, learning about levers, learning about wheels, pulleys, and then combinations of these machines.

These are all steps in accomplishing your major goal. If you keep in mind that your major goal is learning about simple machines, you have a "hook" on which to hang everything else. Read the following passage from the beginning of a science unit on simple machines. It makes the point that machines are used to multiply the force you can exert with your muscles.

Machines Multiply Force

In the beginning, all machines started as extensions of the human body. That is, machines are simply tools to assist the muscles of your arms, legs, and back. The unit explains how people use their brains to multiply the power they can exert and let machines do the heavy work they cannot do unaided.

Setting Goals

The author is telling you that your goal when reading this unit should be to see how machines multiply human force and power. If you keep this goal in mind, you will be aware, when you come to study complicated pulleys, that you still want to find out how this machine multiplies your muscle power.

Pulleys and Work

When you use a combination of a fixed and moveable pulley, the resulting machine is called a block and tackle. The mechanical advantage of such an apparatus is determined by counting the ropes that run between the pulleys. You do not count the rope you pull with since this merely changes the direction of the force, it does not add to it. So in the illustration, if you are able to exert a force of 100 pounds with your muscles, the block and tackle will multiply the force by four, enabling you to lift a load of 400 pounds.

100 pounds of force x ropes = 400 pounds.

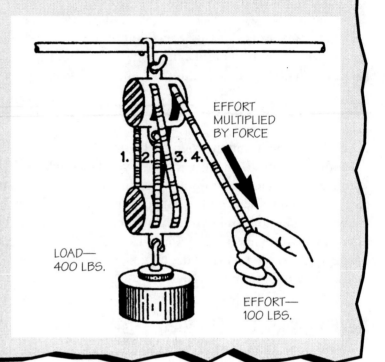

EFFORT MULTIPLIED BY FORCE

1. 2. 3. 4.

LOAD— 400 LBS.

EFFORT— 100 LBS.

This passage near the end of the unit is more complicated than the first passage. Your goal here is to understand pulleys. But your *major* goal is still to understand how machines multiply the force you are able to exert yourself. If you keep this goal in mind as you read, it helps keep your thinking on track and makes the lesson easier to understand.

In order to accomplish your own reading goals, it is very helpful to think about what the author's goals were in writing the book or article you are reading. The reporter who wrote the article about the dam set out to provide readers with information about a dangerous situation. The science writer's goal was to teach you about simple machines and how they work.

Because you know the science writer is trying to teach you something, you look for step-by-step explanations. Because the reporter is expected to give you facts about the dam so you can make a judgement, you look for those facts. If the reporter just tells you about the troubles of the people who were evacuated, you would have to change your reason for reading the article. If the science writer tells you how his grandfather used pulleys to hoist hay into his barn, it is no longer science but history, and you would have a different purpose for reading.

When you read a humor columnist in your newspaper, like Art Buchwald, your goal would be to examine his opinions about an issue. You would not read his column to obtain facts. And it helps to know that most political writers are trying to convince you that their view of things is correct. In this case your goal would be to compare one opinion with others and then make up your mind.

Setting Goals

Exercise A

Read the feature story carefully. Think what your goals might be as you read the article. (There can be more than one goal or reason for reading.) What is the *writer's* goal? Complete the exercise on page 72.

Let's Eat More Rabbit

by Susan Yancy

The annual convention of the Alternative Foods Council, meeting in Nashua, Nova Scotia, had the theme "Eat More Rabbit." The members were united in their efforts to make people aware of the benefits of including more rabbit in their diets. They make a good point.

Rabbit is cheaper and better for you than beef or pork. Rabbits require less feed per pound than other kinds of meat, and they are ready for market faster. In these ways they are like chicken. And if they were raised in the same quantities, they would be just as cheap.

Like chicken, rabbit has less fat and many fewer calories than pork, beef, or lamb. People should eat more lean meat, and rabbit is very lean. It's healthy and economical. Because rabbits take up very little room, they can be raised in almost any backyard. It's hard to raise chickens because they are messy, smelly, and noisy. Rabbits, on the other hand, are neat and quiet.

According to Barney Krasden, chairman of the Alternative Foods Council, Americans have been reluctant to eat rabbit because of the "Easter Bunny syndrome." People picture rabbits as part pet, part myth. Rabbits are cute and cuddly. Children listen to the tale of Peter Rabbit at mother's knee. And rabbits bring candy baskets on Easter morning. This makes

What? Me worry?

Photo by Stan Sherer

people queasy about eating rabbit meat. We don't have the same feelings about cows and chickens and pigs. These are thought of primarily as food sources, so it doesn't bother us to see them in the supermarket.

Rabbit, however, has always been a delicacy in Europe. And many hunters enjoy eating wild rabbits, although these little fellows are tough and gamey

tasting compared to domestic rabbits raised for food.

To help sell rabbit as food, the Alternative Foods Council is offering a cookbook by Nancy Davis called *Rabbit Cookery*. It contains more than 40 recipes for rabbit, including Thanksgiving rabbit roast, hearty stews, and even party hors d'oeuvres. Ms. Davis says there are no recipes for Easter eggs.

Setting Goals

Exercise A (cont.)

1. What is the author's goal in writing this article?

  ( ) a. To entertain you with an amusing story.

  ( ) b. To sell a new rabbit cookbook by Nancy Davis.

  ( ) c. To tell of the benefits of using rabbits for food.

  ( ) d. To hurt meat-producing industries.

2. If your reading goal is to understand why many people have avoided eating rabbit, what information would you pay most attention to? _____

  _____

  _____

3. If your goal is to understand why rabbit may be desirable to include in your diet, which information would you pay most attention to? _____

  _____

  _____

4. Suppose your goal is to decide for yourself whether or not you would like to eat rabbit. Tell in a few sentences how this article has affected your feelings about eating rabbit. _____

  _____

  _____

  _____

  _____

Now Try Your Newspower

Keep a "Reading Goals Diary" for at least one week. Each time you sit down to read, no matter what you are reading: newspaper, schoolbook, magazine, comic book, whatever— enter your goals for reading in the diary. After you have finished reading, tell why you think you have accomplished your goal, or why you have not.

An entry in your diary might look like this:

Reading Geography book—"The Countries of Africa."

Goals:

- To learn the names of the countries
- To learn their locations in Africa
- To learn the major products of each country
- To remember the information and review for a test

Accomplishment of goals: I found the names of the countries and wrote them down. I found the location of each country and made a note of this next to the name of each. I found the products of each country in my reading and listed these next to each country. I then had an outline which I used to study for the test, which I passed with a grade of B+.

Setting Goals

Practice Using Your Newspaper

Use articles from your newspaper to accomplish the following goals:

- Form an opinion about a problem that affects your city.

- Entertain yourself.

- Learn how to do something (cook a special dish, fix a lamp, for example).

For each of the stories you use, do the following:

1. Copy the headline of the article.

2. Tell what your goal is for reading the article. For example—"My goal is to get information to help me decide about the need for higher taxes in our city." "I would like to find a better recipe for chocolate chip cookies than the one I use now." "I want to find out why the Chicago Cubs are having a losing streak this year."

3. Tell why you accomplished your goal in reading, or why you did not. Examples: "I did not accomplish my goal because the writer did not offer enough solid information about why the Cubs are losing." "This seems to be an especially good recipe because... etc." "As a result of reading the article I have learned... etc."

Article 1: Opinion About a City Problem

Headline _____

Reading Goal _____

_____

Accomplishment of Goal _____

_____

Article 2: Entertainment

Headline _____

Reading Goal _____

_____

Accomplishment of Goal _____

_____

Article 3: Learn How To Do Something

Headline _____

Reading Goal _____

_____

Accomplishment of Goal _____

_____

Setting a goal for yourself is the first step in learning to think as you read. You recall that the way you decide on your reading goal was to ask yourself questions: Why am I reading? What do I want to accomplish?

You continue the thinking process throughout your reading by asking yourself still more questions. Here are some of them:

- Who or what is being written about?

- What is happening? Why is it happening?

- Why or how is this information important?

- How is the information related to other things I know?

- How do dates or the order of steps in a procedure help in understanding the reading?

- Where are the events of the reading taking place? Is this important to understanding the reading?

- If I don't understand something, *exactly* what is it that I don't understand?

- Is there something more I would like to know about the subject that isn't in the reading?

These questions are different from the questions you find on a test or at the end of a chapter in your textbook. *These are questions you ask yourself* that help you take an active part in your own learning. No one ever learns by having information pounded into them from the outside. People learn when questions come from inside and answers are actively sought through reading and listening carefully. Following is a feature news story. There are questions in the margin that you might ask yourself as you read. Assume that your goal in reading is to learn something about dinosaurs.

New Dinosaur Exhibit

What is a Paleontologist

What else lived during this time period?

Do dinosaurs eat plants? Do they also eat other animals?

Dr. Jason Owens, a paleontologist at the Newton Museum of Natural History, announced the opening of a new exhibit featuring the skeletons of 12 species of dinosaurs from the Jurassic period, the "age of the great reptiles," 180 million years ago.

The remains of the dinosaurs in the exhibit were all discovered by an expedition led by Dr. Owens in 1983. What is special about this exhibit is that the museum is also able to show the fossilized plant materials discovered with the dinosaur bones that are thought to be part of the large beasts' diet.

"We really don't know why the dinosaurs became extinct," Dr. Owens said. "Perhaps the climate changed or there was a change in the food supply. There are theories about meteor showers or some other catastrophe from outer space. We hope exhibits like these will will keep people's curiosity in the mystery alive until one day it is solved."

Why did dinosaurs become extinct? Even the experts don't seem to be sure.

Asking Questions

Notice that some of your questions are answered as you read the article. Others are not. You find out that a paleontologist is someone who studies the remains of ancient plants and animals. You learn when the Jurassic period was–180 million years ago. This suggests that the history of the earth is divided into periods.

Why did dinosaurs become extinct? This is another unanswered question. It is one of the interesting mysteries of the ages. You might even ask yourself, why do we want to know? Put it this way: Why would we be interested in knowing if a meteor shower or some other calamity caused the extinction of dinosaurs? See if you can come up with some answers of your own.

Why Ask Questions?

If you haven't done it lately... Ask Questions! As far as your study-reading is concerned, here are the reasons for asking *yourself* questions:

- Self-questioning as you read helps you concentrate.

- When you concentrate you understand more and remember more.

- Self-questioning helps you pinpoint exactly the things you don't understand.

- Questioning helps you organize what you know into large blocks of useful knowledge.

- Finally, asking questions helps you think new thoughts and create new ideas.

How to Ask Questions

The kinds of questions you ask vary a bit as you do different kinds of reading. Sometimes you will ask yourself *why* a character in a novel acts a certain way. In science you may ask *how* a process proves a theory.

There are certain kinds of questions that keep coming up and apply to almost everything. They are a good place to start if you are just learning how to ask questions as you read.

Fact-finding questions

Who or what is the subject of the reading?

Why is the information important?

What is happening and why is it happening?

When and where is the action taking place?

Exploring or probing questions

How is the information related to other things you are reading?

How is the information related to other things you already know?

What, *exactly*, do you not understand? This should always be written as a specific question.

When you are finished reading, ask at least one more question simply because you are curious. Then think about possible answers and find an answer if you can.

Asking Questions

Exercise B

Read the newspaper article. Then complete the exercise on page 77. As you read, set goals based on the following questions:

1. What are some goals for reading the article?

2. What are some fact-finding questions you can ask (who, what, where, when, how)?

3. What are some exploring or probing questions you can ask?

Students Are Teacher for a Day

MILTON—Students at Daniel Morgan High School are learning what it is like to be a teacher. For an entire month, teams of students plan, prepare, and teach each day's history lesson. Teacher Anna Mayer holds a "teacher training" session to acquaint students with their new responsibilities and outline the month's course—The Development of a Democratic Constitution. Mrs. Mayer counsels student teachers as they prepare their teaching plans, and she holds classroom critiques of each team's performance. Other than that, the students are on their own.

They find out what it means to prepare a lesson and present it to the class. They prepare and grade quizzes, and handle all the chores that are part of teaching. Student teachers take attendance, deal with make-up quizzes and other hand-outs, and grade homework. And, of course, they teach the day's lesson.

Says sophomore Kevin Miller, "I used to think teaching meant walking into the classroom, talking for a while, and then giving a test. Maybe you holler at the kids occasionally to keep them in line.

"My partner Sean McGill and I spent more than a week preparing our lesson plan. Then the day we taught, kids kept asking questions so we had to go back over things. We didn't have nearly as much time to teach as we thought—what with taking attendance, fielding requests for passes, notes from home, and I don't know what all."

Mrs. Mayer points out that there are many benefits for students in this month-long program. "The greatest benefit," she says, "is that the student-teachers learn respect. Respect for the preparation that teachers do for each class. Respect for the teaching task itself. Kids often give student-teachers a hard time-until they have to teach themselves. Then they find out what it's like to take flak when you're trying to do a serious job. They're easier on me, too, afterwards," she said.

Junior Marie St. Clair says she will never forget the history of the Constitution as long as she lives. "It's different when you read your history book to get by, and when you read it to teach the lesson to others. You know they're going to ask questions, so you have to read more than just your history book. You have to really bone up on your subject. Even then you get stuck."

But everyone agrees it's a challenge that's worth the effort. Student teacher Carla Ruiz summed it up by saying, "It makes you feel like you have really done something important in class—not just sat there. And you find out there's a career challenge in teaching that you didn't think about before."

Asking Questions

Exercise B *(cont.)*

1. Write your goal for reading the article. _____

_____

_____

2. **Fact-finding Questions**

   a. What is the article about?_____

   _____

   _____

   b. Where is the action taking place? _____

   _____

   _____

   c. Why are the students teaching? _____

   _____

   _____

   d. Who is the teacher in charge? _____

   _____

   _____

   e. What do students have to do? _____

   _____

   _____

   f. What do students get from the experience? _____

   _____

   _____

3. **Exploring or Probing Questions**

   a. Why does it take a student a week to prepare to teach one class? _____

   _____

   _____

   b. What does a teacher do besides teach? _____

   _____

   _____

   c. Write a question of your own. What would you like to know about students teaching at this school that you are not told in the article? _____

   _____

_____

Asking Questions

Practice Using Your Newspaper

1. Select a rather long article from your newspaper that you find interesting. Copy the headline of the article and write down your goal for reading the article. Then answer the questions.

   Headline _____

   Reading Goal _____

   Who or what is the article written about? _____

   _____

   Where does the action take place?_____

   When does the action take place? _____

   Why is the subject important? _____

   _____

   Tell something you already know about the subject. _____

   _____

   Tell of one thing in the article you don't understand, or something you would like to find out about the subject that is not in the article. _____

   _____

2. Find an article that describes a new machine or a new procedure. Examples: a new car, a computer, a defense system, a medical development. Copy the headline and write down your goal for reading the article. Ask three questions about the article.

   Headline _____

   Reading Goal _____

   Question 1._____

   Question 2._____

   Question 3._____

Now Try Your Newspower

Read one or more newspaper articles about a subject that is in the news a good deal lately. This might be about defense, taxes, a foreign war, a medical event, a local scandal, etc.

Pretend you are a Congressman or the local district attorney investigating the situation. Make a list of questions you would like to ask witnesses.

Examples: How much will this cost? Is it safe? How do you know it's safe? How much study has gone into the project? Will this affect anyone's rights? How can we keep this from happening again?

If more than one person chooses the same topic, compare your lists of questions.

Finding Relationships by Asking More Questions

You have probably guessed by now that asking yourself questions as you read is a way of thinking. Finding answers is learning and understanding. The more you think to ask, the more you will learn and understand.

It is said that learning feeds upon itself. What this means is that you can use knowledge you already have to learn new things. For example, suppose you want to build a small storage shed for your bike and other things. You may take knowledge you already have of building a birdhouse and relate it to building your shed. You use your knowledge of math to adjust the proportions of the tiny structure to fit a larger one. You use other knowledge you have acquired to make plans to keep the floor dry in wet weather.

This process of relating one piece of knowledge to another is an important part of thinking. It is also called using your imagination. By relating old knowledge and new experiences you learn new things. It works exactly the same way when you read to learn.

In order to find relationships in your reading, you have to ask yourself these kinds of questions:

How are the facts and ideas related to things I already know?

If you are reading about the Native American Wars in America, you will want to think back to what you already know about the coming of white men and how conflicts arose. If you are reading baseball averages, you will want to think of what you already know about decimals and percentages that you learned in math.

How are facts within the reading related to one another?

In textbooks you will find that information is presented in a special order, or in steps. Each step in presenting new information is related to what has gone before. That is why if you skip steps in reading your textbooks, you can become confused.

How are actions related to results? This is called a cause-and-effect relationship.

You read in your newspaper that a man was driving drunk. This is a cause. The effects may have been an accident and a injury or an arrest. The British levied a tax on tea. This was a cause of the revolt (the effect) in the colonies.

What new thoughts come to you that are related to what you have read?

Now you put all the relationships together to come up with ideas of your own. New knowledge you create yourself comes from making new relationships. This is called using imagination. It is the most important result of being an educated person. Because you have learned many things in the course of your education, you can use your imagination in new and productive ways.

Finding Relationships by Asking More Questions

Read the following article. As you read, try to be aware of how new ideas come to you by combining what you read with things you already know about exercise and health. Then complete the exercises on page 82.

Swimming is Top-Rated

by Raoul Moyano

According to specialists in sports medicine, swimming is one of the best sports for all-around body conditioning. Swimming improves body flexibility, strength, and coordination, and provides a solid aerobic workout. When you swim, you use all your muscle sets, which results in a better developed body.

Swimming is one of only a few body-building and aerobic sports that don't pose a threat of damage to body parts. Jogging can cause serious knee and foot injuries. The sudden starts, stops, and impacts of tennis can cause a variety of joint injuries. Even aerobic dancing can cause muscle pulls and strains.

In swimming, on the other hand, the body is supported by water so there is less, rather than more, strain on joints and muscles. This means you can exercise for long periods of time, giving your heart and lungs a good workout without threatening other body parts. Muscles develop long, smooth lines rather than the big bulges you develop in pumping iron.

Because swimming does not place stress on joints, it is the exercise of choice for people suffering from joint injuries and bad backs. Shoulder and hip joints that are stiff and sore out of water can often be exercised rather easily while swimming.

How are the facts and ideas related to things you already know?

You have certainly heard a good deal about exercise and body building. Everyone knows something about swimming. You start comparing what is said in the article with things you already know or have heard elsewhere.

How are facts within the article related to one another?

Swimming is related to body conditioning. Swimming is compared to other sports. Swimming is related to people in need of exercise who have back or joint injuries.

What are some cause-and-effect relationships?

Swimming has the effect of improving body flexibility and providing an aerobic workout. Swimming causes you to develop long, smooth muscles.

What new thoughts come to you that are related to the reading?

Perhaps you know people who have a fear of water. You realize that the information in the article cannot apply to these people. You might ask, what do people do who don't have regular use of a pool? You may think, I'll suggest this to my father, who has had a bad back for years.

Having asked and answered all these questions, you will have begun to think far beyond the information provided in the article. You are thinking for yourself—even creating new knowledge or new uses for the knowledge you have learned.

Exercise C

Read the news article and answer the questions that follow. As you read, think about relationships as they were discussed in lesson 3.

Navigators Lead the Way

Ancient people were good at using the sun, moon and stars to guide them when traveling long distances. This worked pretty well on land. But at sea, when clouds might cover the sun and stars for days, it was very easy to get lost.

Vikings used to carry birds on their voyages. They would release the bird hoping it would see land and fly towards it. One reason that world exploration didn't start in earnest until the 1400's was that there were no good, reliable navigation aids until then.

The science of navigation grew rapidly in 300 years after Columbus made his famous voyage. By the 18th century it was a high science. Sailing ships explored and charted all the oceans of the world with great accuracy.

Then there were no more real advances in navigation until the middle of the 20th century. Radio, then radar, and finally, communications satellites quickly added more convenience and accuracy to navigation. Computers now do many complicated navigational problems that a navigator had to do with head and hands before.

Women first became military navigators in 1977. Until well past the middle of the century, women weren't even thought of for navigation training. It was assumed they couldn't handle the

Air Force officers arrive at navigation school to begin training.

math and physics it required. These were considered "male areas of study."

But women began to serve with distinction as mathematicians and physicists just before and during World War II. During the war, women pilots ferried bombers to Europe, which required great navigational skill. Finally, in 1977, the first women were admitted to the Air Force navigation training school.

In the years since 1970, barriers have come down for women in all math and science-related fields, not just in navigation. Careers in engineering, biotechnology, economics,

computer science, and new branches of science just opening up are available to anyone willing to invest the thought and effort required.

The new navigation is in space, of course. As more and more people and their machines embark on travels through space, more and more navigators will be needed to prepare the routes and lead the way.

Finding Relationships by Asking More Questions

Exercise C *(cont.)*

1. In talking about navigation the article goes all the way from Vikings to space travel. Write a sentence telling how these two things can be related in your thinking. _____

   _____

2. Which one of the following expressions best relates to all of these words that were mentioned in the article: navigation aids; radio; radar; communications satellites?

   ( ) a. ancient history

   ( ) b. women's issues

   ( ) c. star gazing

   ( ) d. finding directions

3. Tell how you think each of the following is related to navigation studies:

   a. Mathematics _____

   _____

   _____

   b. Physics _____

   _____

   _____

   c. History _____

   _____

   _____

4. From your history, science, scouting or camping experiences, you probably know about a very common navigation instrument that isn't mentioned in the article. What is it? _____

   _____

5. Write a sentence or two telling one thought or idea of your own that comes to you as a result of reading the article. _____

   _____

   _____

   _____

   _____

Finding Relationships by Asking More Questions

Practice Using Your Newspaper

Find newspaper articles that you can relate in some way to subjects you study in school. Explain how the news articles are related to the school subjects. Find one newspaper article for each subject.

History

Headline _____

What the article is about _____

_____

How I relate the article to history _____

_____

Science

Headline _____

What the article is about _____

_____

How I relate the article to science _____

_____

Math/Arithmetic

Headline _____

What the article is about _____

_____

How I relate the article to math _____

Now Try Your Newspower

Find an article in your newspaper where you can see a cause-and-effect relationship. For example: A sports article tells about a team acquiring a new player. This is a cause. The effect may be that the team has a better chance at a championship. The effect may be stated in the article, or you may predict it yourself, if you wish. Another example: An article tells that rainfall is far below normal. This is a cause. The effect may be that crops are doing badly or water is being rationed.

When you have chosen your article, do the following:

- Tell the subject of the article.
- Tell what you identify as a cause.
- Tell a related effect described in the article.
- Tell what you think may be other effects of the action or event's that are mentioned in the article. Use your imagination to think of as many possible effects as you can.

Asking questions as you read means judging, or *evaluating*, what you read as well as finding facts and ideas. Here are some questions which will help you evaluate what you read.

- Are you satisfied with what you have read? Have your questions been answered?
- Who is talking? Can you have reason to believe this person?
- Is the reading only facts, or does it present someone's opinion?
- Are there questions raised by the reading that need to be answered?
- Do you need to consult other books on the subject to find your answers?
- Are there questions you want to discuss with your teacher or someone else?
- Does something important seem to be missing?
- Is an explanation (how? why?) complete, or is it left hanging?
- Is the reading slanted toward one viewpoint or another? Does it seem deliberately false or misleading?

These are the kinds of questions you should keep in mind as you judge, or evaluate, what you read. Read the following articles and evaluate them by asking questions.

Cancer Research Promising

GRAYSPORT—Dr. Raelynn Kahn, speaking before a panel of cancer researchers, said that early detection and new ways of using radiation and chemical therapy have resulted in higher cancer cure rates. Moreover, people are more aware of the warning signs of cancer, and doctors are better trained to recognize symptoms and act quickly.

Dr. Kahn's findings were supported by other members of the panel. Statistics were offered to show that patients diagnosed early had a higher cure rate than those diagnosed later. They also pointed to figures which prove that more people are diagnosed as having cancer than ever before. "No, I don't think that means there is more cancer," explained Dr. Kahn. "I think it means that in the past, many people died of cancer before they knew they had it."

Can you believe Dr. Kahn? In other words, is she an authority in the field? As she is presented to you in the story, Dr. Kahn does seem to be an expert.

This story offers both fact and opinion. The opinions were those of cancer researchers and doctors who specialize in treating cancer. They have gathered facts from their research. You would probably decide you could trust their opinions.

Evaluating What You Read

You might still raise other questions about this article. Questions like, have all sides been heard from? Were any other conclusions reached by the panel? How do cancer patients feel about the new treatments?

Read and evaluate the next article in the same way.

UFO Sightings Reported

ASKEW—For the past two weeks, residents of rural Askew have observed an eerie pattern of lights which begins shortly after midnight and continues well past 2 a.m. Townspeople claim the lights come from unidentified flying objects—UFO's.

"We've notified the Air Force and they keep saying 'no comment,'" says Larry Jones, an Askew farmer. "I say they know a lot more than they are letting on."

"People should take this thing seriously," urges Gerry Anne Knight, whose property adjoins Jones'. This could be an invasion from outer space or something. Everyone in town has seen these lights and everyone has the same opinion. Even the experts agree with us. We know these are UFO's and we want some protection."

This story raises many questions. Who says the lights in the sky are UFO's? Where are these lights seen? How many people saw them? What experts in weather and astronomy also evaluated the lights?

False and misleading evidence can be difficult to discover at first glance. Sometimes people draw conclusions hastily. They do not consider other possible explanations. Perhaps the lights in the sky were the northern lights, produced by weather conditions. This fact should be considered before you decide that UFO's exist.

Witnesses should be carefully evaluated. Perhaps the strange lights were first seen by small children telling each other "space stories" while camping out in their backyard. Mr. Jones and Ms. Knight say "everyone has seen them." But who is "everyone?" What did they see?

Sometimes a writer may quote an "expert" without telling who that expert is, "Experts confirm that the lights were indeed UFO's." Critical readers would want to know, "What experts? What are their names? What makes them 'expert'?"

Some people want to believe in UFO's, so they overlook flimsy or unsupported evidence. But if what you want is the truth, then you will ask hard questions to find it.

Evaluating What You Read

Subjective and Objective Writing

Writing is called *objective* when a writer presents you only with facts. In objective writing the writer does not tell you feelings or opinions. Nor does the writer try to make you feel the way he or she does about a subject. Here is an example of a news article that is written *objectively*:

Accident Blocks Interstate

LEYDEN—One person was killed and three were injured when a tractor-trailer went out of control and overturned on I-75 at about 2:30 p.m. Three cars following the truck were unable to stop in time and crashed into the wreckage. The northbound lane of the I-75 was closed to traffic for more than three hours. Names of victims have not been released pending notification of next of kin.

All you read in this article is an account of what happened. What you think about the accident is up to you. The writer has not tried to influence you. But now read another version of the same accident that is written *subjectively*. This time the writer is clearly playing on your feelings by revealing her own feelings:

Slaughter on Interstate

LEYDEN—A tractor-trailer that was clearly overloaded and traveling at an excessive rate of speed overturned on I-75 at 2:30 this afternoon. While the driver of the truck walked away with scratches, three cars couldn't avoid hitting his rig, leaving one of his victims dead and two others badly injured.

It is plain that the writer feels the truck driver was at fault. She is playing on your feelings with her *subjective* style of writing to make you feel the same way. She uses leading, emotional words—*slaughter* and *his victims*. She states that the truck was overloaded and speeding without telling you how she knows. This seems to be her opinion.

The differences between objective and subjective writing are not always this clear. The author of a history book may try to be objective and present you only with facts. But writers are human, after all, and have feelings. Sometimes their feelings get into their writing and you get a mixture of objective and subjective writing.

You need to be cautious in judging, or evaluating, subjective writing. You should be aware that the writer's feelings and opinions are in the writing and judge it accordingly. Do the facts support the writer's opinions? Is there another way of looking at the same facts?

Newspapers try to make the difference between objective and subjective writing very clear for readers. News articles present facts and are objective. Columns and editorials present opinions and are almost always subjective. Knowing the difference helps you to evaluate what you read.

Evaluating What You Read

Exercise D

Read the following news story. Then complete the exercises on page 88.

Living Dinosaur Photographed

CEDARBURG—If seeing is believing then we must all believe. And, unbelievable as it may seem, a real, living brontosaurus was seen and photographed by 30 year-old photographer Peter Clemens.

"I was shooting at an abandoned construction site on the outskirts of Cedarburg," explains Clemens. "There was no one around for miles. I heard loud, heavy sounds, and before my very eyes, this enormous creature stepped out of the woods and walked across the site.

My first impulse was to turn and run. I felt like I was in a sci-fi movie, or in some sort of time warp. I thought I might have been transported back to prehistoric times!"

Clemens credits his instincts as a photographer for getting the picture. "Despite my fear, I just kept shooting pictures. I only had about four more shots on my roll and they are all of the dinosaur."

Experts confirm that the reptile in Clemens' photograph looks like a brontosaurus. "This dinosaur commonly reached a height of twelve feet and a length of over 60 feet," said a noted paleontologist.

"The dinosaur I photographed was at least that big," said Clemens. "I deliberately photographed it next to a road sign for comparison."

Dinosaurs have been con-

A live dinosaur?

sidered extinct. However, some people believe that it is possible for small groups of dinosaurs to have survived in isolated areas. One resident, who lives several miles away from the abandoned construction site, said that quite often she hears the sound of a large, heavy animal near her home. "It's always at night and I don't see well in the dark," says eighty-year old Mary Joachim. "But it is not the kind of sound that would be made by a dog— even a very large one. This animal is much heavier than that."

"Parts of this state are so remote that I have no trouble believing dinosaurs could live here undetected," says Clemens.

"After all, no one can explain Big Foot or the Loch Ness monster, but they still exist. I'm aware of the impact of my picture. I may have set modern science on its ear! I would have liked to capture the creature. But obviously I couldn't do it on my own."

Clemens says that the dinosaur roamed the site for about fifteen minutes and then disappeared back into the forest. "I stayed rooted to the spot for about five minutes, just waiting," he explains. "Then I realized the dinosaur might come back with a meat-eating friend, so I jumped in my car and took off.

It was real," insists Clemens. "I saw it."

Evaluating What You Read

Exercise D *(cont.)*

1. The article states that "seeing is believing." Does this statement always apply to photographs? Why or why not? _____

_____

_____

_____

2. The story quotes experts who confirm the size of the brontosaurus. Does this prove that Clemens actually saw one?

   (   ) a. Yes   (   ) b. No

Explain why you answered the way you did. _____

_____

_____

_____

3. Does the statement of Mary Joachim prove Peter Clemens' story is true? Tell why it does, or why it doesn't. _____

_____

_____

_____

4. Clemens points to the Loch Ness monster and Big Foot as evidence that dinosaurs may still exist. What is wrong with this evidence? _____

_____

_____

_____

Evaluating What You Read

Practice Using Your Newspaper

Read a fairly long report of a news event in your newspaper. Be sure the article is a report of a news event and not the writer's opinion about an event that has been in the news.

Answer the following questions that will help you evaluate the article.

1. Headline _____

2. What is the article about? _____

3. Think of at least one piece of information the reporter does not tell you that you would like to know. _____

_____

4. Where did the reporter get the information for the article? (A police report; a "source" or "spokesperson"; a person who is named; etc.) _____

_____

5. Do you feel you have gotten enough good, honest information from the article to learn something? Explain your answer. _____

_____

_____

6. It is very difficult for a reporter to be entirely objective when writing a news story (just reporting facts—no feelings or opinions).

   a. Copy one or two sentences from the article where you think you detect the way the writer feels (subjective writing)._____

     _____

   b. Briefly, tell what you think the reporter's feelings are. _____

     _____

   c. In your opinion, is the reporter being fair and accurate in reporting the news? Explain why you feel as you do. _____

     _____

Now Try Your Newspower

- Read a section of your history book that is one or two pages long. Try to read a complete article (an account of a baffle and its results; a law passed by Congress or Parliament and what it meant; why explorers went exploring; etc.)

- Evaluate the article in the history book by answering the same questions that you answered about the news article above.

Talking with Max Kirkwood

Lots of complaints about homework and taking tests:

Dear Max:
I try to study, but here is what I have to put up with. My sister plays the piano—not too good. My other sister plays the flute worse. Sometimes they play together, but most of the time they're fighting. Then I get into a fight trying to get them to be quiet. My mother says I should just study and mind my business. How can I study?

Tammy Davidson

Dear Max:
I consider myself a good student. I'm on the hockey team in winter and the baseball team in spring. I'm also good enough to be in our school's Student Tutor's program. We help younger kids with their work.

My problem is I never seem to have time to study. I'm tired after practice and games, and the young kids take up a lot of time I need to study myself. My grades are slipping. I don't want to give up sports. And I like helping the little kids. What should I do?

Keith Stolz

Dear Max:
Math is my worst subject. English is my best. Other grades range from good to so-so. I used to work on my math a half hour most nights, but it didn't do any good. My Mom says she was never good in math either. It must run in the family. But now I have to pass math to stay on the baseball team. Any ideas?

Mickey Fromer

Dear Max:
I hate tests! I think they're unfair. I'm good in class, I do my homework and get good grades on that. I get good grades on reports. But when I take a test my head is like a sieve. I can't remember anything. What can I do? And why should I have to take tests in the first place if my class work is good, and all my other work?

Rebecca Reskowski

To the student using this book:

I'm willing to bet you have all had problems like these students have—and you can probably add a few to the list. So I'd like you to be the ones to make suggestions for solving the problems instead of me.

Write down your suggestions. Then tell about a major problem you have yourself with homework, studying, and tests.

Finally, discuss all the problems—including your own—with other kids, with your parents and with your teacher.

Max Kirkwood

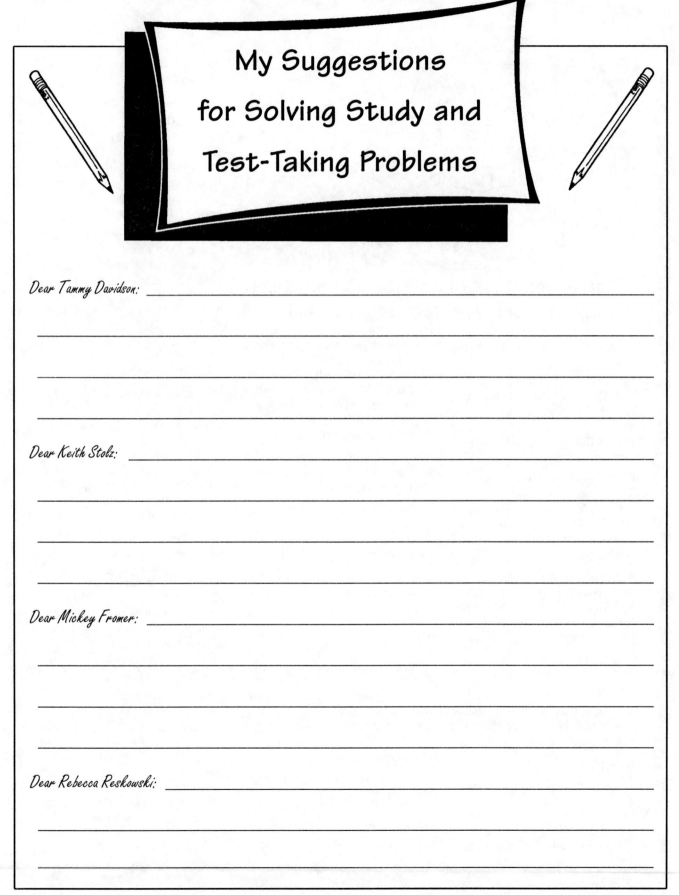

My Suggestions
for Solving Study and
Test-Taking Problems

Dear Tammy Davidson: _____

_____

_____

_____

Dear Keith Stolz: _____

_____

_____

_____

Dear Mickey Fromer: _____

_____

_____

_____

Dear Rebecca Reskowski: _____

_____

_____

Talking with Max Kirkwood

What do you think of dress codes for school?

...I was thrown out of class. Can you imagine?

Part A

Dear Max:

What do you think of dress codes for school? I thought that was something that died 20 years ago. And I thought everybody knew by now that it's what's inside a person that counts, not how he's dressed.

Our school recently adopted a dress code. I was sure they couldn't be serious—just something to appease parents and the school board. So I ignored it, of course.

The upshot was that when I came to school as usual in my fatigues and T-shirt I was thrown out of class. Can you imagine? In this day and age!

Independent in Saginaw

Dear Independent:

Yes, I can imagine. But for a case that is just the opposite of yours, read the next letter.

Dear Max:

Part B

I like to present a good appearance. So I spend a lot of time in the morning on makeup, and I dress to the hilt. I wear designer dresses and use jewelry for accent purposes. The other day I chose a set of bangle bracelets to highlight a new outfit. My teacher told me to get rid of the awful clanking, and while I was at it to wash my face. I was never so mortified!

They want you to dress nicely for school, and when you do that's what you get.

Dressed down for dressing up in Atlanta.

Dear Dresser:

It doesn't just happen to girls. Read the next letter.

Dear Max:

I earn pretty good money after school, so I can buy a lot of my own clothes. What I buy is the latest. I mean up-to-the-minute. I watch men's fashions in the mags and newspapers, and I'm always the first in school to wear what's hot in New York or L.A. I'm a trend setter in fact.

And what do I get for my trouble? Ridicule! Not just other kids make fun of my clothes, but teachers too. They're worse than the kids. I suppose it's because they grew up in the 60's when anything went. Do they want me to dress like a slob in old fatigues and a greasy T-shirt?

Fashion plate in El Paso

Part C

Selecting the right clothes to wear isn't easy. It's a skill that has to be learned just as you learn most other things. And that's one of the reasons behind dress codes in school—to help teach you what is appropriate in your workplace.

Some of the defense mechanisms people use to excuse inappropriate ways of dressing include these: It doesn't matter how you dress...I dress to be comfortable...you can't tell a book by its cover...they're jealous of me... I'm modern, they're old fashioned...I dress to be me...I dare to be different...etc.

The word appropriate is a key word for choosing an outfit. You wouldn't crawl under a car in a good sweater and slacks, and you shouldn't wear greasy fatigues to school. Bangle bracelets and dramatic makeup may work well at a party, but they are a bit much for the workplace—school, that is.

Part D

The "fashion plate" in Texas misses the point that most fashion fads that make a splash in the tinsel towns never make it in the rest of the country. Most are publicity gimmicks to push the reputation of a designer, or they are bait for those who "dare to be different" and don't care how they waste their money.

Clean-neat-appropriate. Those are the buzz words for the successful dressing. If your outfit is all of these you'll rarely have to worry about what other people think. Beyond that, most people, both kids and adults, can benefit greatly from reading a good up-to-date book on dressing for success.

End–of–Book Skills Review

Reviewing With Max Kirkwood

Some of the following words and expressions that were used in Max Kirkwood's column may be new or unfamiliar. Decide what the words mean by using techniques you learned in the lessons. Write the meanings in your own words.

Sections of Max Kirkwood's column are labeled Part A, Part B, and so on. The exercises are labeled the same way to help you locate the words so that you can see how they are used in complete sentences and paragraphs.

Part A

1. dress codes _____

2. adopted _____

3. appease _____

4. upshot _____

Part B

5. dress to the hilt _____

6. for accent purposes _____

7. bangle bracelets _____

8. highlight _____

9. mortified _____

10. trend setter _____

11. ridicule _____

Part C

12. appropriate _____

13. defense mechanisms _____

14. inappropriate _____

15. you can't tell a book by its cover _____

16. dramatic makeup _____

Part D

17. fashion plate _____

18. fads _____

19. tinsel towns _____

20. publicity gimmicks _____

21. reputation _____

22. designer _____

23. buzz words _____

Answer Key

Chapter 1

Exercise A (Page 10)

1. It's difficult to get into veterinary school because there are so few places available in freshman classes. This is because there are not many veterinary colleges.

2. Other subjects you would study if you wanted to become a veterinarian include chemistry, physics, and math.

3. A veterinarian with an equine practice treats horses.

4. An orthopedic surgeon could provide the most expert treatment for a pet with a broken leg.

5. If your dog hides under the bed frequently and growls at you, you could say he has a *personality problem*, and you might take him to an animal *psychiatrist*.

Exercise C (Page 20)

1 Example: What is the job of the sailor's at McMurdo Sound? (answer: To deliver supplies to Marble Point)

2. Paragraph Examples
Example for Paragraph 1: What is the greatest risk in traveling across Antarctica? (answer: getting delayed by bad weather)
Example for Paragraph 2: What does the convoy do during a blizzard? (answer: They call a halt and relax in their shelter)
Example for Paragraph 3: What is the biggest problem facing convoy drivers in Antarctica? (answer: fatigue)

3. Name two things to look for when examining a crack in the ice. (answer: signs of age and frost; whether it is pulling apart)

4. Example of an essay question: How can the world as a whole benefit from the research at Marble Point?

Chapter 2

For questions that ask for your opinion or your own words there can be more than one correct answer. In these cases an example of a correct answer is given.

Exercise A (Page 31)

1. b, c	3. d	5. c
2. a	4. a	6. a

Exercise B (Page 36)

1. a	3. d	5. b	7. c
2. c	4. a	6. c	8. a

Exercise C (Page 40)

1. c

2. "good things that happen when an animal does what it's supposed to."

3. "something unpleasant that follows a wrong move"

Exercise D (Page 43)

1. b

2. A summit meeting is a meeting of the top leaders of each country

3. c

4. A "springboard for peace" is a way for enemies to "jump" over their differences to arrive at an agreement.

Exercise E (Page 47)

1. a and c	4. b
2. d	5. enthusiasm
3. b	

Chapter 3

Exercise A (Page 52)

1. c	3. a
2. b	4. c

Exercise B (Page 57)

1. Some of the facts about a baobab tree include huge trunk; sometimes trees are lived in; cloth is made from the bark; medicine is made from the leaves; the gourdlike fruit can be eaten. (There are other facts as well).

2. c

3. a. A sequoia is the taller tree. It has a huge trunk, second in size only to the great sequoias of California. It's not very tall for its great width, however…

   b. It has a huge trunk, second in size only to the great sequoias of California. It's not very tall for its great width, however…

4. A baobab is likely to be most useful to people in developing countries.

Exercise C (Page 62)

1. c

2. asphalt desert; destroying Maple Street

3. Maple Street was named for the trees growing there. A decision has been made to cut down the trees. Maple Street can't handle even present day traffic. Drivers have been injured crashing into trees.

Exercise D (Page 66)

1A. Example of a correct answer: The advertiser wants you to infer that you have already won $50,000–just send in the coupon to collect.

1B. A correct inference is that you will be eligible to win $50,000–just as everyone else who received the advertisement will be eligible.

2. b

3. b

4. Often–means sometimes, or not always temporary relief–a short time minor aches–not very strong

Chapter 4

Exercise A (Page 72)

1. c

2. You would pay most attention to the "Easter Bunny syndrome."

3. You would pay most attention to information about rabbit as economical and a healthy food to eat

4. Any thoughtful answer can be correct.

Exercise B (Page 77)

1. Examples of good answers: Your goal may be to learn about an unusual teaching method; to form an opinion about this way of teaching; to think about asking your teacher to try this in your school.

2. a. The article is about students who teach a history class.

   b. The action takes place at Morgan High School in Milton.

   c. The students are teaching to find out what it is like and what it takes to prepare a lesson and conduct the class.

   d. The teacher is Anna Mayer.

   e. Students have to prepare a lesson, teach it, give a quiz, take care of class business and keep order.

   f. Students learn to appreciate how much work and preparation there is in teaching a class.

3. a. A student must read more than the lesson to be ready to answer questions. It takes time to study a lesson closely and prepare a quiz about it.

   b. A teacher has to prepare lessons, teaching materials; take attendance and tend to other office business; keep order, etc.

   c. Any thoughtful answer should be considered correct.

Exercise C (Page 82)

1. Example of good answer: All navigation seems to be related to some sort of travel.

2. d

3. a. Mathematics is needed to work navigation problems that relate to such things as speed and distance.

b. Such things as an aircraft's speed and the speed and direction of wind, which are governed by laws of physics, have to be taken into consideration in navigating.

c. Anyone studying navigation would want to know how the science developed over the years, and that is a study of the history of navigation.

4. A compass.

5. Example: Everyone uses simple forms of navigation: landmarks in the neighborhood help you find your way home; people use road maps and figure how far a trip will be; you may use a compass on hikes.

Exercise D (Page 88)

1. Photographs may be the result of special effects created by the photographer, or there may be something left out of the picture. So, seeing is not always believing when it comes to photographs.

2. No. Simply saying that dinosaurs existed once doesn't prove that they still exist today.

3. Mary Joachim did not say she saw anything. Her opinion is the result of her imagination, or what she thinks if might have been.

4. These monsters (whose existence has never been proven) have nothing to do with the dinosaur Clemens says he saw.

Page 93

Part A

1. dress codes: rules for what clothes may or may not be worn.

2. adopted: accepted or made a rule.

3. appease: satisfy

4. upshot: result or conclusion.

Part B

5. dress to the hilt: all dressed up in high fashion.

6. for accent purposes: bring out or emphasize.

7. bangle bracelets: large, solid bracelets that bang against each other when worn together.

8. highlight: The way the word is used here means the same as accent, above. It means bring out certain features.

9. mortified: extremely embarrassed or embarrassed to death.

10. trend setter: someone who starts a new trend or style.

11. ridicule: make fun of.

Part C

12. appropriate: correct, just right for the occasion.

13. defense mechanisms: ways to excuse or apologize for oneself.

14. inappropriate: not right or not correct for an occasion.

15. you can't tell a book by its cover: you can't tell what is inside something by looking at its outside.

16. dramatic makeup: makeup that is heavy as if put on to play a part or call attention to oneself.

Part D

17. fashion plate: like a picture of a clothes model in a magazine. A "plate" in this case is a picture.

18. fads: styles that come and go quickly.

19. tinsel towns: glamorous cities.

20. publicity gimmicks: a trick used to gain publicity or the notice of the public.

21. reputation: what people think of a person.

22. designer: someone who designs or creates new styles in clothing.

23. buzz words: key words or catch words you want to pay attention to.